PRAISE FOR THIS BOOK

'An often chilling series of recollections gleaned from ... colleagues in Special Branch and CID, many of whom have never spoken before about the Troubles.'

Belfast Telegraph

'A most powerful and unique insight into the world's most dangerous job in policing in the 1970s and '80s.'

Henry McDonald, *Observer* and *Guardian* Ireland correspondent

'Fascinating and intriguing stories from inside a police force on the front line of inter-communal conflict and violence, and a reminder of the high price paid by its officers.'

Peter McDermott, *Irish Echo*, New York

'Murders, robberies, terrorism, information gathering ... paramilitaries and the black, defensive humour that kept people sane are all here in abundance ... Compelling, frank and often disturbing.'

Policebeat: Magazine of the Police Federation of Northern Ireland

'If you like dark and inappropriate humour – pick up this book. Great read, very moving and funny.'

David Feherty, columnist and broadcaster

'The RUC was a hero organisation to some and a villainous one to others ... a book like this helps to separate fact from fiction and reinforces that at the heart of our history, human beings make the war and make the peace.'

Joe Cushnan, *Belfast Telegraph*

'This book of real RUC insider anecdotes makes a delightful alternative to other accounts of policing the Troubles. It has, of course, the best possible sources – the cops themselves.'

Hugh Jordan, *Sunday World*

A FORCE LIKE NO OTHER

The real
stories of
the RUC men
and women
who policed
the Troubles

Colin Breen

·THE·
BLACK
·STAFF·
PRESS

If you are a former member of the RUC and have a story to tell, please do not hesitate to contact me at aforcelikenoother@gmail.com

First published in 2017 by Blackstaff Press
an imprint of Colourpoint Creative Ltd
Colourpoint House
Jubilee Business Park
21 Jubilee Road
Newtownards BT23 4YH

Reprinted 2018, 2019, 2020

Colin Breen has asserted his right under the
Copyright, Designs and Patents Act 1988 to be
identified as the author of this work.

Printed and bound by CPI Group UK Ltd, Croydon CRO 4YY

A CIP catalogue for this book is available from the British Library

ISBN 978 0 85640 972 1

www.blackstaffpress.com

Some names and identifying details have been changed
to protect the privacy of individuals.

I dedicate this book to the memory of police officers everywhere who have made the ultimate sacrifice, and particularly to the 302 members of the Royal Ulster Constabulary who died during the Troubles.

'For peace we served.'

In memory also of my brother Robin Breen, late of the Toronto Police Service.

Introduction

In 1983, Interpol named Northern Ireland as the most dangerous place in the world to be a police officer. The figures bear that out: between 1969 and 2001, 302 RUC officers were murdered, and over 10,000 were injured, 300 of them left disabled or seriously injured. Almost 70 officers committed suicide. Since then the RUC has become the PSNI, and that change, combined with the passing years, has made the gathering of these accounts by those who were there even more important.

This is the story of the men and women who policed the Troubles, told for the first time by them and in their own words. Over a number of years, as well as writing down my own stories, I interviewed former RUC, Special Branch and CID officers. I know that none of them would have spoken to me if I hadn't been a former member of the RUC myself.

A Force Like No Other is the frank and remarkable story of our everyday lives, of what it was like to be a cop: never hanging police shirts on the washing line; lying to children and friends about the job; checking over your shoulder and looking under your car for bombs; always on the alert for things out of place. At times, it stretched us to breaking point.

Despite the dangers, many felt their time in the RUC formed the best years of their lives. The humour, often bleak and dark, and the camaraderie that bound us together are everywhere in these accounts. That humour acted as a protective shield. 'Normal people' might find it unsettling but it worked for us. The humour – or a bottle of whiskey – was the only possible antidote to the death and horror we lived with every day.

The camaraderie that existed in the RUC is as strong amongst its former members today as it ever was. We ran towards danger, knowing that we all had each others' backs, creating an unspoken, invisible and unbreakable bond that will stay with us to our graves. When we see one another, it's like we spoke yesterday, even if it has been years.

I started this project thinking that I would put together a humorous book about weird and wonderful encounters between police officers and the public. However, it became immediately apparent that the officers I was talking to had much more important things they wanted to talk to me about – stories they hadn't even been able to tell their families. Several became very emotional and upset while they talked but were determined to give their accounts.

There were a few who wanted to contribute but couldn't – even thinking about the past brought back the demons, sleepless nights or nightmares. Ironically, there was also one officer who said he had far more trouble policing the peace than he ever had at the height of the terrorist campaigns. He had become used to living on high alert and was hooked on the stress and adrenaline – he simply couldn't handle peace. Others found solace in a bottle and sadly paid the price.

The three sections of the book reflect the RUC's basic eight-hour shift pattern: Earlies, Lates and Nights. It was tempting to group the stories into neat chapters or to follow a chronological structure, but I hoped that using our shift pattern to shape the book would give the reader a sense of the unpredictability of a typical day for an officer on duty. You literally did not know what you would be facing when the phone rang or the radio crackled into life.

When I approached the people who tell their stories in this book the first thing I told them was that they would be anonymous. I knew this would be important to them because, while all of them have retired, I was aware they would still be sensitive to potential risk even after all this time. It's our default setting. I still have to sit facing the door in restaurants or bars to the point of asking people I'm with to move. Consequently, many names have been changed to protect identities.

I deliberately set out to get stories that would provide a good cross-section of policing around Northern Ireland as the job can vary greatly between rural and urban stations, and between internal departments such as CID, Special Branch and so on.

Apart from the removal of some police jargon for clarity, I have recorded the stories directly as they were told to me, to retain their immediacy and authenticity. Many of the officers that I interviewed were visibly reliving the experiences they recounted. While I have tidied up and streamlined stories here and there, I have remained faithful to the integrity of their individual voices. These are their stories and I wanted their voices to tell them.

When the violence erupted in 1968 the RUC had a couple of thousand members. As violence took hold, the force quickly expanded, reaching thirteen thousand at its peak. It was, to say the least, a very steep learning curve as officers tried to keep pace with fast-moving events on the streets, for which they were totally unprepared. Despite the obstacles, the RUC managed to solve 50 per cent of murders committed by loyalists and 30 per cent of those carried out by republicans.

The RUC evolved from a small rural-type service to the most internationally respected anti-terrorist police force in the world, whose former members still train other forces across the globe.

Ultimately this book is the human story, told from many personal perspectives, of how ordinary people cope in extraordinary times. None of the men and women of the RUC would have chosen the circumstances in which they found themselves, but they did their best with the cards they were dealt. Their stories show us how a career choice shaped, changed and ruined lives – but also about how the human spirit triumphs in the darkest of moments.

Earlies
07:00–15:00 hours

07:01 – North Belfast

When you finish your training it doesn't take long to find out there's a very different world out there from the one you're used to.

When I came out of the training centre, I was stationed in Belfast. Being from the country, I was used to everybody being nice and friendly, always having time for a chat.

I got sent to the city for my first station – in a very busy area, which had suffered greatly during the Troubles. Belfast was a bit of a war zone and I don't mind admitting it, I was more than a bit nervous. But excited, keen to do well.

The first morning on duty, I was put out on the beat with an older peeler to hold my hand and show me the ropes. That was standard practice to break you in gently and get you to see a wee bit of the area. We hadn't gone a hundred yards from the station and I noticed this wee lad walking towards us, school uniform and bag on. All set for my first encounter with the public, I waited until he was right in front of us, looked down at him with a big friendly grin on my face and said, 'Are you heading off to school then, son?' He looked back up at me and replied, 'Where the fuck do you think I'm going dressed like this?'

That was my introduction to the public!

07:06 – Rosemount Police Station, Londonderry

As the person telling this story sat in front of me, reliving that fateful day, I could see the events he was talking about were as fresh in his mind as if they had happened a few minutes ago. He started by drawing me a map of the area, to help me get a clearer picture of what exactly had happened as his patrol car travelled to Rosemount Police Station at the end of a shift. This event occurred just two days before Bloody Sunday in 1972. He was in no doubt that it may have created a mood that contributed to those tragic events.

We came along here [Infirmary Road] and turned right on to the Creggan Road to go down to the station. Brooke Park runs all the way down on our right and the Creggan estate on our left.

The first gunman opened fire from this entry. The first thing I noticed was white dots appearing across the windscreen. Then Peter's head exploded. He was in the front passenger seat. I was sitting behind him. I knew he was dead. Bits of him were splattered over me.

Our car kept moving forward. The driver was trying to zigzag. Two more gunmen opened up on us from Helen Street. The car got past the junction and, as it did, Davy slumped forward and towards me. He was sitting in the middle, I was on his left. The driver was still trying to zigzag to get us out of danger. If he had been hit we all would have died. He managed to get the car on down the road to Rosemount and stopped. I got out and went round to the passenger door behind the driver. I opened it and Charlie sort of came with it. He was badly wounded. I got him out of the car and carried him to the station. There was a wee wall round it and I set him down behind it and went back to see about Davy. As soon as I saw him, I knew he was gone.

He had been shot in the back. The rounds had gone through the boot of the car and the seat before hitting him. I had swapped places with Davy in the back of the car about twenty minutes before the attack. It just wasn't my time to go.

I went back to Charlie at the wall and carried him into the station. The army arrived and took him to hospital in one of their ambulances. In the station, one of the bosses spoke to me for a couple of minutes. After an hour, I was told to go on home. It was never mentioned to me again. I took a few weeks off and was transferred to another county.

No one even took a statement from me. But I was just a cub and assumed others knew what they were doing.

Two other things I remember about it, even after all these years. We really had no way of defending ourselves. We had one old .38 revolver and it had to be kept out of sight in the glove compartment. We had also repeatedly asked for a set of keys to the gates to Brooke Park. There was a road through it, which would have given us a much safer route to the station. I always wonder why we were never given them.

Decades later, the Historic Enquiries Team contacted me and, as much out of curiosity as anything else, I agreed to meet them. After we'd discussed the actual shooting they wanted to know if any suspects' names had been bandied about at the time. They asked who I thought was involved, and I said, 'You tell me.' When pushed on this, one of them said, 'The Deputy First Minister, McGuinness himself.' I told them it was known in police circles that there were two Thompson submachine guns in the city at the time and McGuinness – who had stated he was second-in-command of the IRA then – was known to keep one as a personal weapon. Two Thompsons were used in the murder.

07:39 – Rural Police Station, County Tyrone

Route clearances were carried out daily, particularly in rural areas, to determine as far as possible that no improvised explosive devices or landmines had been planted during the night on any of the main arterial roads leading to or from the police station. The intention of the paramilitaries was to set these off by remote control, murdering everyone in a passing police patrol.

One morning, the boys were out on the ground, clearing some of the routes. The main Drumnakilly Road was next to be cleared. Steve was the inspector, I was in the office and he was heading into Omagh Station for a meeting. He was only outside Carrickmore about a mile at the most when he came across one of the foot patrols. It was being led by a sergeant named Bob.

The reality of the route clearances was that you only ever had four or five personnel due to availability, and the way they did them was like an inverted V. You had guys out front on the high ground – the top of the V. If there was some terrorist sitting with a transmitter to detonate a bomb the people on the high ground would come upon them – neutralising the threat – while there was no one on the road to be hit by the blast, as they would have been there first. That was the inverted V system. Simple but effective.

Bob the sergeant had been out on a flank for whatever reason and he had been crossing over a barbed wire fence when he saw what looked like a bit of fishing line. What he did next was rather foolish, I suppose. There are no rivers or lakes around there, so a fishing line was completely out of place.

He caught hold of this line and gave it a really good yank. Luckily, whatever way he did it, the line snapped. Then he walked back along the fence towards the road to where the fishing wire had been leading. This was just as the inspector was driving past. The inspector stopped and they both spotted a concrete water main, the cover of which had been split into two halves. It was a common enough sight in the countryside. As they were having a look at it, they noticed what appeared to be fresh footprints round it.

The next thing, I got a call from the inspector asking if I could get a crowbar and bring it out to them because they wanted to move this two-part lid to see into the drain to be sure it was safe. It was so ludicrous when you think back – madness. But of course I couldn't find a crowbar. I searched all around the station and all I could get was the metal part of a pickaxe. But there was no shaft on it. It could act, though, like an improvised crowbar.

When I found them I jumped out of the car and headed towards them in the field. I could see the other boys were up on the high ground giving cover to us with rifles. I had been stationed there a couple of years at this stage, and really should have known better than to be doing this. The next thing, a woman left her nearby house, got into her car and took off. She was in a hurry and very agitated. I thought it was suspicious but I was still so preoccupied about not having found a crowbar.

We jammed the pointy end of the pick in – if you had had a crowbar you would have slid it across. Across the road they had been building fencing along the road and the workmen had left a pile of those 4x4 paling posts. I suggested if we lifted the metal lid a wee bit more we could put a couple of these posts in, which would help with the light.

Myself, the sergeant and the inspector were down on our knees in this field trying to see what's going on. Steve, the inspector, then decided he didn't want to get his hands dirty any more. Me and the sergeant did all the spadework, literally. We managed to get the cover lifted further up and I was trying to look down into this thing. I thought I saw something that looked a wee bit like insulating tape, blue tape or something. I never thought it through. The next thing the inspector's down on his hunkers and he goes, 'HOLY FUCK, RUN!' That wasn't something we needed to be told twice. Off we went and boy did we run!

I was off weekends back then. I used to work five days on and two off. It was a Friday, so I'd be going off for the weekend. I'm not superstitious, but as it happened, it was Friday 13 January! I couldn't wait to get away. I headed for home as soon as I got back to the station. Later that night I was out down the town having a beer with some mates when this big fellow who worked in Carrickmore Station as well walked in.

He was off on his rest days, and he came up to me in the bar and said, 'Did you hear the news?' I said, 'No, what's happened now?' He said, 'You know that suspect device thing you were at this morning? It was a 600lb land mine.' 'You're fucking joking?' He said, 'No, I'm afraid I'm not.' The terrorists had taken fright when they saw the police coming towards them doing the formation. They didn't run the wire but they had like a clothes peg with a dolly pin in it and the two connectors. Their plan was they'd pull it out with the fishing line, which would complete the connection. But they had panicked and scarpered. Luckily for the sergeant, when he pulled the line, it broke so the dolly was still in the clothes peg, and it didn't go off.

With hindsight I have no doubt that the woman who left her house and drove away when she saw us at the drain cover knew exactly what was going on and that there was a bomb there. She was happy enough to have us blown to smithereens but she didn't have the stomach to see or hear it. It was pure luck we survived.

07:41 – CID Office, Musgrave Street Police Station, Belfast City Centre

There was a murder I remember going to round in Hill Street in the cathedral area of Belfast. Back in those days the tramps about the town used to lie down anywhere to sleep. Difference was this boy was lying dead with his pants down round his knees.

He had a gash at the back of his head. His wallet was missing but we found it round the corner from the body. I thought we had a murder case. He had a newspaper stuck down his pants, which was a bit of a mystery. We thought, could he have fallen over maybe, slipped back and knocked himself out? Maybe somebody took the wallet? We started to do a few enquiries, myself and another detective. The paper could have been for insulation from the cold of the ground, if he had been sitting there. Maybe it was a red herring.

We got information that there was a woman who worked in a club in North Street who may have seen something. It was a homosexual club. The other detective said to me, 'I hope nobody sees us going in here.' We were having a bit of a laugh. The first person we saw behind the bar was a boy that I knew from Bangor, who had been involved with the Daffodil Club, a homosexual ring in Bangor.

The woman I wanted to talk to wasn't on that night, he told us. 'She is on tomorrow night. If you want to call round after six she'll be here then,' and he set us up a pint. Our enquiries didn't throw anything up and the case was parked. Any evidence we had was inconclusive. Years later, long after I'd left Musgrave Street, a girl walked into the station and reported it was her then-boyfriend had killed the old tramp. She and her boyfriend had been together all those years but recently had fallen out. She made a statement saying that she had been with him when it happened and added he had fled the country. He had robbed the old boy who had fallen back and hit his head off the wall on his way to the ground. And I used to pay no attention to all this stuff about a woman scorned!

07:59 – Uniform Patrol, Oldpark Police Station, North Belfast

The armoured Land Rover was the standard patrol vehicle if you were based in Oldpark. The cops in the Land Rover always went out on a Sunday morning to the Antrim Road Station canteen and got a fry to take out with them and eat in the vehicle, while parked up somewhere.

One of the crew, he was an observer, had just got into the vehicle, set his cap behind him and was watching the traffic going by when he saw this character driving who had nearly caused a major accident. He hadn't waited at the stop sign or something. The cop said, 'I'm going to have this fucker.' He put his cap on, went out, and stopped the driver with the intention of giving him a bit of a bollocking. He was talking to the man, telling him off, nodding the head and wagging the finger. Giving it the full nine yards!

You could see the smirk starting on the driver's face, and it growing the more animated the cop got. The next minute the car driver just burst out laughing, just couldn't hold it in any longer. It was like when you laugh in church and you just can't stop. Unbeknown to the policeman, the other guys in the Land Rover, when his cap had been lying in the back, had broken off half a sausage and stuck the sausage under the crown on the cap. All the driver of the car was seeing was this sausage wagging up and down at him. The cop doing the scolding was getting more and more cross because he was not being taken seriously, and the man just couldn't cope with being told off by a red-faced, finger-wagging policeman with a sausage wobbling around on his head! He was not best pleased when he found out about the sausage!

08:00 – Antrim Road Police Station, North Belfast

Atrocities were happening daily – there was just no let-up. It was early one morning at the Antrim Road Station, I was having a cup of coffee at about 8 a.m. I'd gone in early to catch up with some paperwork while I had a bit of peace before the phones started ringing.

I was just thinking about what file I should tackle next when a massive explosion shook the building. I thought it must be the front gate being attacked – which wasn't an uncommon occurrence then – so I ran out fearing the worst. It actually turned out it was a bomb a bit further down the street towards the Waterworks, on the left-hand side of the Antrim Road. I ran down towards the house the bomb had gone off in to see if I could help. When I got there, this guy was lying there with his arm missing, and I mean missing. There was just a hole with bits of flesh and shattered bone sticking out. He was bleeding badly; he was a mess. There were other injuries as well but his arm was the worst as far as I could see, there was blood everywhere.

What had happened was the Prods [a slang term for Protestants; used in this instance to refer to loyalist paramilitaries] had planted a bomb at the house owner's front door; a booby-trap bomb meant to get him when he left the house. But one of his workers had arrived at the house to collect him and, sadly for that guy, he set the bomb off. I had to administer first aid as best I could and then other people started to arrive and began to help. When the ambulance arrived, they took over.

That was me going into work one morning early. I went in to get a cup of coffee and ended up trying to put somebody's arm back together, and covered in blood from head to toe. So I went back home, showered, changed and started again.

08:49 – Strandtown Police Station, East Belfast

There was a man who came to us because money was going missing from his office. It was a solicitor's office. After questioning, it appeared the only person who would have access to the office was this wee elderly woman who cleaned the place. She had worked there for some time and was from the Shankill Road.

Jimmy Thompson and me were tasked with investigating. We decided that we would set the place up. We'd get the blue dye stuff and coat some money with it. You put it on the notes and if anyone touched or took anything coated, their hands would go green when they came into contact with water. It took days to get off.

We'd wait until the cleaner had finished and the minute she came out we would be waiting for her. While we were waiting, after an hour or two, these two girls came out of the office so we went over and asked them who they were and what they were doing. They confirmed they were in the office cleaning the place, but one of them, the top of her nose was green. She had rubbed her nose after lifting the cash.

It turned out the wee woman wasn't well and was scared of losing her job. These two girls were her friend's daughters, who said they would fill in for her and keep her in work. They stole the money. When they saw the green stuff on their hands they got disinfectant and scrubbed their hands. But one of them had scratched her nose and that's what caught her. What puzzled me was that some cash had been left in the office. There was about fifty punts – the Republic of Ireland currency then. I wanted to know why they didn't take it. Their attitude was that they were Prods from the Shankill and they didn't want to touch Fenian money, but they were glad to take the rest.

09:06 – Strand Road Police Station, Londonderry
Paddy McNulty was a detective constable in CID in Derry and a good friend of mine. I bumped into Paddy one evening when he was trying to move a snooker or billiard table out of Waterside Station. It wasn't the easiest thing to shift, so I decided to give Paddy a hand. As always he was in great form. We were chatting away, having a laugh as we struggled to move the table, and he promised to buy me a pint afterwards.

We were both into cars like a lot of young lads. He had a bright orange Ford Escort. I was keeping him going about the bright colour of the car, which would have been trendy, but I told him you'd need a pair of sunglasses to look at it!

Then he said, 'Maxi,' as he called the car, 'is going in tomorrow for its first service.' I asked him, 'Where's it going to?' He said, 'Desmond's on the Strand Road.' I said to him, 'Are you sure that's wise, Paddy? You're stationed on the Strand Road, that sounds a bit risky to me.' He tried to reassure me by saying, 'The car is registered to my uncle, he has a different surname, he's on my mother's side, so everything is going to be okay. I have no worries about it.'

I was on the early turn the next morning and just after 9 a.m., I got the call to go to Strand Road; there had been a shooting. We arrived at the scene and Paddy was lying shot dead in his car just outside the service area at Desmond's garage. The car was peppered with bullets. It was horrendous … that was hard to take in. I'd been talking to and having a laugh with him less than twelve hours previously. Just an ordinary family man with two young sons aged three and five, trying to earn a living like the rest of us.

Raymond McCartney and another guy [Eamonn Mac Dermott] were convicted of his murder. The passage of time, well you never forget, but it becomes easier. But then two or three years back there, Raymond McCartney and the other fellow appealed the conviction. I was coming home from work and I heard on the news that the conviction had been overturned.

It just opened it up all over again. It was like a bit of steel going through my heart. It all came flooding back to me. McCartney had been the OC [officer commanding] of the IRA in jail and had taken part in the dirty protest and hunger strike in 1981. But I have to accept the law. That's the law that I have upheld my entire life. The court found that the conviction was unsafe. But it's these things that bring the horror of what people do back into your head.

09:11 – CID Office, Musgrave Street Police Station, Belfast City Centre

The events below occurred in the 1970s when Belfast city centre was sealed off with security gates to prevent car bombs getting in. People and cars entering the area were searched. At night the centre was locked up with only one gate open for access.

Not too long into my career in CID, my detective sergeant walked into the office. I was sitting at my desk. It was a Monday morning and he throws me down this wee plastic bag with what looked like a finger in it. I thought it was a joke finger. He said, 'I want you to find out who owns that.' I thought he was taking the piss. 'It was found just below the turnstile at the security gates in Chichester Street.'

I just thought to myself, where am I going to start with a finger? I rang round the hospitals, feeling like a bit of an idiot to be honest, asking if anybody had been admitted with a missing finger. Nobody! Then I thought of your woman Candy Devine. She was working in the Abercorn Cabaret place in the centre of Belfast. I knew her but more importantly she also had a popular show on Downtown Radio. I spoke to Candy and asked her if she would appeal over the airways on her show, asking anybody who had lost a finger to come to Musgrave Street police station, sort of half-joking too, because I did feel like a bit of a dick. Bizarrely enough, I got a phone call soon after from Mountpottinger police to tell me that a person had been admitted to the hospital in Dundonald, just outside Belfast, with a finger missing and he was having surgery as we spoke.

He alleged he had been kidnapped by the IRA and taken away up round the Short Strand area in Belfast, where he'd had his finger chopped off. I thought this was too much of a coincidence.

I went down to the hospital, not knowing what to believe, but sure enough there was your man lying with his hand strapped up. I said to myself, this boy's at his work here, compensation is setting in. I knew by looking at him. I just threw the finger down and said, 'Do you recognise that?' You should have seen his face. I told him, 'I'm investigating this and let's not waste anybody's time. I don't believe you – you said you'd lost your finger, that it was chopped off. That doesn't look chopped off to me.'

I told him that the finger was found in or around the bottom of Chichester Street in the city centre and I said, 'If I have to start investigating this and you are acting the candy man and applying for compensation I will make sure you'll get nothing and you'll maybe end up inside as well. Now I'm being clean with you, tell me the truth.'

I knew by the look on his face that he had something to tell me. I said, 'Let's start at the beginning.' He said, 'I'll tell you what happened. I was in the club down in Chichester Street, you know the wee club that used to be upstairs, where George Best's mother and father used to drink. It's above the jewellery place. Well, I came down and when I went out through the turnstile at the end of the control zone, I remembered I'd left my cigarettes. I couldn't very well go back, I'd have to walk the whole way round the segment area in High Street and back up round again, in around Arthur Street and up to get the cigarettes.'

He decided he'd climb over the top of the gates. There were spikes to stop anybody doing what he was trying to do. The drink wouldn't have helped, and he had slipped and fell. As he lost balance, his wedding ring caught on the spike and it ripped his finger off. Of course he went on home; he said it didn't cause him any pain and there wasn't much blood. The drink in him kept him going.

Then he wondered what the hell he was going to do and how was he going to explain this to the wife – that not only had he had lost his wedding ring but his finger with it! That's when he came up with his master plan. He thought of compensation coming in as well. He made up the story about being taken away and having his finger chopped off during his kidnap. When he admitted everything, I could have charged him with wasting police time. But I think he had suffered enough for one day.

09:12 – Special Branch Office, Belfast

In the early 1990s, I was at a function in Palace Barracks in Holywood. It was a summer evening, June, and we were in our summer suits. It was a champagne and cocktails function, and it was all very nice. Myself and another senior officer were talking to a woman that I know very well. Her husband is a very good friend of mine. The adjutant came over and said, 'Gentlemen, the Lord Justice would like to have a word with you, please.'

We went over and the commanding officer was talking to Lord Justice Kelly. It turned out the Lord Justice had said to him, 'Are there any RUC men here?' He had replied, 'Yes, there are two,' and he had asked to talk to us.

I think that the Lord Justice wanted to speak with us for no other reason than that he couldn't make small talk with all these army officers. He lived locally and had been invited to the function by the commanding officer at the time. It was the one and only time I met him, a fascinating man, not a man given to any small talk, as many of these boys aren't. He told us that he had been the person who heard the appeal of one of the Supergrass trials. He'd heard all the evidence that was given verbally, read through all the notes, which was a huge part of it, and then he'd hired a cottage in the Lake District for two weeks and he went off with his wife to study everything to reach and write his verdict.

He said he went through it all with a fine-tooth comb and he decided that the convictions were indeed safe and satisfactory and that the sentences should stand.

He then came back to Northern Ireland on the Sunday and he was due to deliver his verdict on the Monday afternoon. On the Monday morning he was called in by the Lord Chief Justice Lord Lowry, who told him that the British government was no longer prepared to run with the Supergrass system. He was told that he had to let them all out and he told myself and my colleague that he had to go in and give a verdict that was the complete opposite from what he had been planning to do.

He said there was no question that the evidence was more than sufficient to convict them but the government wasn't prepared to run with it and that's the only real proof that I have of the government interfering with the judiciary although I'm sure it happens all the time. That was straight from the horse's mouth.

09:19 – Special Branch Office, Belfast

Here is an earlier example of government interference, of which I'm certain, involving [names a prominent republican I will call Mr A]. Mr A was charged with carrying out a major bombing outside Belfast. He was looking at sixteen years in jail and I know that [names two Sinn Féin members I will call Mr B and Mr C] were putting pressure on the secretary of state. Mr B and Mr C played on Mo Mowlam. They told her Mr A was a man who carried the Maze prison and was very influential in keeping the prisoners on board with the peace process, and that if he was now anti-peace process, the prison would swing against the peace process to support him. She was also told that would be the end

17

of the entire peace process, and her and Tony Blair's pet project would be ruined, probably forever.

I don't know what happened next, except for the fact that when it came to the sentencing Mr A got four years and because of the time he had served on remand that was him back out on the streets. I know afterwards he kept saying to people, 'There I was thinking I was gonna go down for sixteen or eighteen years and the next thing is I'm skipping down the steps of the fucking courthouse.'

What happened was that Mo Mowlam, under pressure from her Sinn Féin contacts, which was a deliberate tactic on their part, got in touch with an appropriate higher authority in London and said, 'There are several decades of more violence here unless you can find a way to get this boy out.' As a consequence, Mr A went 'skipping down the steps' immediately after being sentenced.

I am certain because I saw all the information coming in from all the different republican sources across the Province. Such was the infiltration of the republican movement we were receiving details of all their planning and the debrief which took place after their meetings with officials during the process. Sinn Féin had a tactic of asking for things that they knew couldn't be delivered and then they would slip in one which they knew was doable. The government would by this stage be so pleased to have a request they could meet they would fall over themselves to deliver. They might as well have invited us to their debrief at every, and I mean every, level.

I'm certain based on information received that that's what happened in that case but I have no direct proof the way I do have with the Lord Justice earlier. Based on my many years' experience the exact same intelligence was coming from so many different sources, both human and electronic, for it to be wrong.

09:37 – CID Office, Antrim Road Police Station, North Belfast

One of the other incidents from north Belfast that always puts a smile on my face came from Victor Williamson at Antrim Road. We were interviewing a wee housebreaker that got caught burgling a house during the night. We went into the interview room and this guy was stinking. I mean it was really bad, his feet were honking. His solicitor was sitting beside him.

I was a detective sergeant and Victor was a detective constable, so we are starting to sound the guy out to see if he was going to talk. The interviews were recorded, and the next thing I heard was Victor saying for the benefit of the tape, 'This is DC Williamson leaving the interview room.' Up Victor got and out he went. I didn't know what was going on, and I'm going, what's happening here, like, where's he away to? About fifteen minutes later, he comes back in and says, 'This is DC Williamson re-entering the interview room.' He has this aerosol air freshener in his hand and starts spraying it under the table at this prisoner's feet. All you can hear on the tape of the interview is the sound of an aerosol. You could see the solicitor thinking, what's going on. Victor just said to the prisoner, 'You ARE fucking stinking.' And the interview carried on as if nothing had happened.

09:58 – Uniform Patrol, Finaghy Road, West Belfast

We were standing on the bridge at Finaghy Road North, on the outskirts of Belfast. We had set up a checkpoint. I was at the top of this bridge with a Sterling submachine gun, facing the traffic coming in from Andersonstown, giving cover to the rest of the patrol. I was getting a bit bored. The next thing, this guy came walking up the road towards us. I thought I'll just stop him for the craic, to pass the time. I struck up a conversation – 'How are you?' –

planning to fill in a C11 form [sighting report] and amuse myself a bit. I did the usual procedure: 'Where are you coming from?' He said, 'I'm just coming down from the Lisburn Road.' I said, 'Where do you live?' He lived up in Owenvarragh Park, in Andersonstown. I'm wondering what he was doing on the Lisburn Road. 'Are you just out for a walk then?' This was a Sunday morning at about 10 a.m. He says, 'Aye,' and I says, 'Just turn out your pockets there a wee minute, so I can have a look.' I felt there was something not right about him.

Next, I opened his coat and inside was all these letters, post. It definitely wasn't for his house in Owenvarragh Park. It was from where he'd been coming from, some house off the Lisburn Road. I said, 'What are you doing with all this post?' He said, 'Oh, the postman delivered it to our house by mistake. I was just down there to put it into the proper house, but there was nobody there so I was gonna call back.'

I couldn't believe what I was hearing. 'Do you think I'm stupid? Come on, what are you at?' I took him down to the sergeant and said, 'This guy here, he's a part-time mailman it seems.' We wrapped up the checkpoint, confirmed the address and we all hopped into the Land Rover with your man in the back, and around we went to the house. Sure enough, the back door was lying open; he'd burgled the place. I'd caught him red-handed.

We headed down to Lisburn Road Police Station to get the local detectives to sort it out. On the way down he said, 'What do you think will happen to me?' I said, 'Well, it depends on a few things – have you any previous form?' He said, 'I have a wee bit of previous but it was a couple of years ago.' I said, 'You'll likely get charged with burglary. If it's your first offence for burglary, you might be lucky enough, you'll probably get off with a suspended sentence if the judge is in the right mood and your previous form isn't too bad.'

Here he was, 'Is that it? What, nothing else?' I added, 'You'll probably get a fine as well.' Then he quite indignantly said, 'And how am I going to pay a fine?' Joking with him, I said, 'Don't worry, they'll accept cheques.' He said, 'I've no money.' I said, 'Are you not working at all, son?' He just said, 'No.' I suggested, 'Did you ever think of joining the police?' Immediately, with a serious face, he said, 'Do you want to get me shot?' I kept my face straight.

10:05 – CID Office, Lisburn Road Police Station, South Belfast

I was working in CID in south Belfast in the 1970s. There was a lot of burglaries going on in the area and this guy was doing quite a number of them. I had intelligence he had sold a couple of video recorders recently. I had enough to bring him in to question him. Me and another detective jumped into the car.

I was very lucky – the area I was serving in, it was a very highly populated area but ordinary crime was more to the fore, although there was some overlap with terrorism. I pulled up to the front of the house and I noticed all these guys standing out in the garden. They looked like they were all members of his family.

He was from a huge family, maybe fifteen brothers and sisters, plus all their cousins. They were linked to half the area. They were all wearing black armbands and dressed in Showaddywaddy gear, if you remember them, Teddy boys. The brother came over to me and said, 'Thanks for coming.' I said, 'How could I not?' as I tried to work out what the hell was going on.

They let us through the gate and we wandered up to the main door of the house, which was open. The hall was packed with people and I could hear Elvis Presley songs wafting out. There had obviously been a death in the family. The fellow I was after, he was sitting in to the left with an Elvis Presley picture that he'd made when he was in a training centre. It had a lot of wee nails, creating an outline, then you put thread around them and made a picture. It was brilliant.

The living room was packed. The wee critter was sitting and the tears were streaming down his face. I thought, it must be someone very close has died. But then I twigged. It's fucking Elvis, he's having a wake for Elvis. I went in and said, 'I'm awful sorry,' and shook hands with him. He couldn't speak, he was just in tears. On the one hand I was trying to keep my face straight, on the other, I was thinking, fuck Elvis, you're under arrest!

I stepped out for a minute and thought, there's no way I can make this arrest now, the family will go mad and I'll get lynched. I'll ask him to come to the station for an interview when he's feeling better. If he didn't come voluntarily he would be arrested anyway. I went back in and stopped to speak to one of the older brothers and said, 'Listen, I'm going to need to talk to him.' He said, 'What's wrong?' I said, 'He's back at the burglaries.' He said, 'You're not going to take him now?' I said, 'No, I couldn't do that. I never came down with that intention. I came down to pass on my condolences about Elvis.' He said, 'That was good of you. All right, when do you want him?' I said, 'We'll get the funeral over first. Once we get the funeral over, he'll need a little time to grieve.' I set a date for about three weeks later and away I went.

The other detective and I were in stitches. Three weeks later, I was out in a police car. I got this radio message, 'Can you come to the station? There's two people here to see you.' I said, 'Could you tell me who they are?' Turned out it was your man and the brother. I got back to the station and there he was sitting in an interview room. I said, 'Are you feeling any better?' He said, 'Not really,' and he started to cry. I said, 'Look, the reason you're here is I have to speak to you about burglaries.' He said, 'But, but – ' I said, 'But nothing, you know you've being doing them, no use trying to tell me lies. The law may deal with you now.' He said, 'I know, you're right.' The brother had the bag and all for him, knowing he wasn't going home.

I interviewed him. He admitted all the burglaries I had information on, as well as a pile of others. He confessed to get his books cleared – in those days you could TIC them [ask the court to take them into consideration]. So after his sentence he would have a clean sheet.

Sadly, years later that same young fellow got murdered, not because he was involved in anything, because he wasn't a member of any organisation. He was just a burglar. They were just ordinary decent criminals. He was shot by the INLA [Irish National Liberaton Army], it was very sad. His body was found by one of his family. There was a terrible lot of nonsense put in the paper about him, which was rubbish but very upsetting for the family.

I went to the funeral having sought permission from my senior officer. He said, 'In view of the fact that you've dealt with this family for years, I think you should.' There were hundreds there, all criminal types. I was the only peeler for miles, no uniform police presence or anything. It was just a family funeral. I went up and a couple of the boys came down and stood beside me and one said, 'What about you, are you working?' I said, 'No, I'm just paying my respects.' This boy was the most senior member of the family. He hadn't been about at the time of his brother's death. He had been in the Republic of Ireland on holiday, so he hadn't had an opportunity to talk to me.

They were putting the coffin down into the grave. I got thanked by about six boys with leather jackets, organisation boys. They flanked me and said, 'Will you carry the coffin?' and I said, 'Of course.' The eldest brother spotted me and, while the minister was giving his whole thing about dust to dust, he left the side of the grave and ran over, throwing his arms round me and thanking me up and down for coming to the funeral. I said, 'Well, what else could I do?'

It was a foul and cowardly murder. They intended to kill everybody who was in the house. He was living alone at the house which led to him having a whole pile of his mates in. It became a bit of a party house. Then what happened was they were assaulting people who were walking past the house. They'd start asking, 'Are you a Catholic or a Protestant?' They mugged people, taking money off them for drink. These were young lads who were drunken idiots. They weren't organised terrorists but they were Protestants. That was enough for the INLA. The gun team that came across were very heavily armed and it was their intention to kill maybe a dozen. There was no party on when they arrived. The door wasn't even locked. It didn't lock, you could just walk right into the house. Which they did and found him with his hat on as usual.

All of this particular family wore caps, because they were all bald. When you went to arrest any of them in the morning, they always had their caps on, even in bed. He was lying on the settee when the gunmen came in. They just riddled him.

10:57 – CID Office, Tennent Street Police Station, North Belfast

All parts of north Belfast saw a lot of violence and murder. Ballysillan had more than its fair share. There was no shortage of bad boys up there. Some were as bad as you could get.

I charged one guy from there with having killed fourteen people, and I think I only scratched the surface.

I was on duty one Sunday morning in Tennent Street and this guy came in around ten or eleven o'clock in the morning, saying he wanted to speak to somebody senior in the CID. I was the most senior one in, so when the uniform guy rang upstairs, I came down to see what he wanted.

This man reached into his pocket and took out a bit of tissue paper with a bit of bone. He told me he had been walking up the wee laneway around the Boys' Model School in Ballysillan and saw what he thought looked like brain matter. He said the bushes where he found it were flattened down. He decided to scoop this up, including the bone, and brought it all in.

I rang up the boss and told him what had happened. I asked the man if he would mind if I followed him back to the area so that he could show me exactly where he discovered the remains. Right enough, when we got there what looked like brain matter was all over the place. I could hardly believe what I was seeing.

I got in touch with the chief again. Of course he immediately said he was coming in, and in the meantime he told me to go down to the hospital to try and confirm what I thought I had received from the man.

I went down to the Mater Hospital and spoke to one of the duty doctors. In only a few minutes I remember him saying to me, quite formally actually, that he was identifying the bone as a fresh part of a human skull and the other matter was indeed from a human brain. He added that whoever had lost it was dead.

We were looking for a body.

Everyone was brought in to start a murder inquiry. The DMSU [Divisional Mobile Support Unit] search teams were first and they were joined by dog section who started combing the area. Later on that afternoon they found a body. It was male and the back of his head had been blown off by a shotgun. The victim, a wee lad, was a bit slow, God help him, and had suffered from mental health issues. He had been out for a few drinks on Saturday night and had managed to end up in an illegal drinking club up there run by the paramilitaries. That's where the lad had been drinking immediately before his death.

One of the leading paramilitaries in the area at the time was this boy I'll call Number 1. He was well known and a bad bastard. Apparently the young fellow took a drink out of Number 1's glass of beer and laughed about his mistake before he put it down. Number 1 was not the sort of guy to be made a fool of. That one act sealed the young fellow's fate. Number 1 blew his head to pieces all because he lifted the wrong drink.

Number 1 had killed another guy — his body was found but his skull wasn't even recognisable. The reason why he killed him? It was because he asked his wife up for a dance. That's the sort of fucking headcase you were dealing with in Belfast in those days. Everyone was too scared to say what happened, never mind give evidence. It was the same problem on both sides.

Not long after that, I charged Number 1 with the murder of this big fellow [another victim], who must have been about 6' 1". He had been in a bar in Ballysillan. He was having a quiet drinking session. Number 1 was sitting with this other guy and his father — they had been at the dog racing. This other guy's father had just come back from South Africa on holiday, and because he had returned home they were all drinking doubles to celebrate. The old boy was drinking whiskey doubles, and they were drinking vodka chasers.

Something was said and Number 1 gave the old boy a

smack in the mouth and he fell to the ground. His son was that drunk he didn't even object to what Number 1 had done. Number 1 then started to kick the old boy, as he lay on the ground. He was only doing it because he could and assumed no one would interfere, as usual.

The big man, Hugh McFarlane, who was sitting near them at the bar, said, 'For fuck's sake, mate, leave him alone, he's had enough. He's an old man.' Because he was pissed out of his mind, Number 1 took exception to him sticking his nose in and went over to him.

Number 1 was about 5' 8" and this guy was 6' 1". But Number 1 beat the shit out of him. The barman saw all this, all the other people in the place said they had got offside. Number 1 was taking rests, he was beating him that much. The boy never fought back. I don't know why he didn't defend himself, unless he was just so scared of Number 1 and his reputation. Number 1 kicked and beat him, jumped on his head and everything. No one moved a muscle to help him or stop it. When he had finished they just continued on drinking as if nothing had happened with the body lying there until the other two boys said they would take him downstairs.

As an afterthought Number 1 told the boys to go across the road to the builders' yard. The Housing Executive were doing up the houses and they brought back some breeze blocks. They smashed his head open with the blocks to be sure he was dead. Although I'm sure he was dead already.

By the time we got round to Number 1's house, which wasn't long after the murder, he was sitting in his underpants with the fire blazing away with all his clothes in it. We were able to get shoes out which were lying in the bottom of the grate, and got them to forensics.

I had Number 1 arrested and brought to Castlereagh Holding Centre. The next morning, I had the forensics team up to the house. There was a boy and a girl in the place, just kids, but they wouldn't let us in. I had to get one of the boys with me to break a pane of glass to open the door to gain access. There were these wee kids about five or six years old, I'll never forget them sitting there on the settee. It looked like it was the wee girl's birthday as cards were up round the place. Trying to put her at ease I said, 'Is it your birthday?'

She got up, went over to the birthday cards, picked up the cards, put them on the chair beside her, and then just sat, arms folded, not saying anything. Trained not to speak to the police at that age – what hope have they?

I had enough to be able to put a charge to Number 1 with murder, and the other two that brought the body downstairs with manslaughter. I had a strong case and great witnesses. I got the main witness who had agreed to testify into safe custody for his own protection. It was looking good.

The UDA [Ulster Defence Association] was glad to see Number 1 put into custody. They couldn't control him and he was killing people on a whim, a psychopath. That brings police attention and affects their criminal activity and support from locals.

The day after I charged him with the murder it started. Once the details of the savagery of the murder and the use of the breeze blocks got into the public domain, the papers had headlines of 'New Shankill Butchers' and speculated he may have killed fourteen others. The other people charged got drawn into it as well.

About a week later, I was working on the file, getting all the paperwork in order for the trial. The witnesses started getting threatening messages, explaining in no uncertain terms what would happen to them and their families if they gave evidence. After that came bullets in the post, followed by wreaths with their names on them.

One by one, they were coming in with their solicitors saying they wanted to change their statements. The lighting wasn't that good, they didn't really know what happened, they couldn't be sure etc.

I went over to see the assistant chief constable with the director of public prosecutions and my detective chief inspector to discuss the case. The consensus was we were never going to get a case against him, and I had to make arrangements to go to the court and withdraw the charges. I can tell you that was hard to do, knowing full well he was guilty.

After the trial collapsed, he and one of his sidekicks went to London and we heard they were doing 'hits' for London gangs based in Spain. I believe he left London and is up north. Special Branch have been chasing him, saying he's a suspect in a lot of crime over there, including murder.

Sometimes I wonder if they should do DNA tests now, and they might get a case against him. I got the stuff in the fireplace and in those days if you got blood, you could only say the blood's the same – O positive or negative or whatever. But you could maybe nail him now.

10:58 – Foot Patrol with the Army, West Belfast

As the Troubles carried on, you got to know what sort of attacks you might expect when you went out on to the streets. The terrorists evolved as well and they would always be coming up with new ways to try and get you.

Booby traps were one of the regular things you could face. One very simple and clever counter-measure was used by foot patrols. The joint army–police foot patrols in west Belfast used to take a couple of tennis balls out with them. The idea was you would give the local dogs the odd scrap of food, which meant they would be attracted to you when you went out. As the local dogs got to associate you with food, you would then throw the ball for the dogs to chase before you would walk down a back entry or other likely spot for an attack. The dogs would hopefully set off any booby-trap devices that had been left for you.

11:00 – Coffee-time Reflections

There was another time that stayed with me: the murder of David Cupples in Belfast. I had been promoted to detective inspector and was working with one of the MITs [major investigation teams]. It's one of the things I am quite proud about, being in the MIT. I probably investigated over thirty murders, and we cleared them all, except for one.

There are some cases you deal with which are routine. You have to go into automatic pilot, you just go and deal with it, and it's an awful thing to say but you look at the body as if it's a lump of meat. You don't take it personally, because if you took every one personally you'd end up a basket case. And as it turned out I nearly became one.

When I went to the crime team, life was just murders. That's what you dealt with, murder after murder. The one I didn't clear, it was a guy called James McMahon from Lisburn. James was twenty-one at the time of his death. The UDA beat him to death at the River Lagan towpath near the council offices and I was called out to the scene.

I think I got the phone call about half five in the morning, so I got up and went to Lisburn. One minute you are lying in bed with your wife, the next you're out with your SIO doing what you have to do at a murder scene, and in this case a fairly gruesome one.

I was coming home that night at about 11.30 p.m., wanting to get a bit of sleep before having to go back in to attend his post-mortem the next morning at 9.30. I'd been at work for eighteen hours.

I knew I had to get up early because you have to go

and meet the pathologist beforehand and explain the circumstances surrounding the murder.

I was driving past The George restaurant on my way home and my phone rang. It was a senior officer who said, 'Steve, I see you're on call-out this week – there's been a murder in west Belfast and I want you to go.' I said, 'I can't go to it.' He said, 'You're on call-out.' I said, 'I don't care, I've just been up since half five this morning. I'm only just heading home from that murder now and I've to get up early tomorrow morning to do the post-mortem.' He didn't give a shit what I'd been doing.

There had been another deputy SIO brought in to the MIT who hadn't been allocated a team yet. Effectively he had never been physically there but he was there on paper and the only thing I could suggest was that we rang this guy and see if he could attend on my behalf because I couldn't do it.

I had to go home, track his number down and ring the guy and ask him if he minded going to the scene of this murder. Thankfully he said, 'Not a problem.'

I just thought, what is this job coming to, you're like a machine, just one after the other, it's not like it is on television. You don't just attend a murder and walk away, the amount of paperwork that goes on behind the scenes and accountability, everything you do has to be recorded. There comes a stage where you just crack up.

The following year was my turning point, when I thought, I've had enough of this. I've been doing it for twenty-eight years and it's time for somebody else to move in. I went to the boss a short time after it, and I said, 'Phil, I've had enough of this, I'm leaving. I want moved outside this. I've done my turn. In fact, I've probably done more than most people because I spent quite a lot of time in flying squads.' In fairness to Phil, he was setting up a new team, which wasn't going to be dealing directly with things. I got involved in that for the last four years of my service.

It was 2003 that happened. The following year I started to take pains in my chest. I thought I was dying and I went to the doctor. Because of my father dying young, they sent me to do treadmill tests. I was having anxiety attacks at the time too. It was crazy and I was trying to hide it from my missus. At the treadmill test he said there was a bleep and he asked if I wouldn't mind doing an angiogram.

So they checked my heart and everything was okay. In hindsight I never saw it at the time but I was under a lot of stress. It was just an amalgamation of all that happened that I and others were constantly having to deal with. It's unfair to ask you to deal with all that and very much on your own.

People deal with it in different ways. In my thirty-one years of service, if you take out the time I took off when I was shot at, which was about four or five weeks just to get my head settled, if I've been off two weeks in total, that's it. My sick record was exemplary. That doesn't mean to say I wasn't sick, but I felt obliged to go back into work because I was involved in things that nobody else could take over. It wasn't like a uniform job where you're not there, so we'll get another uniform man out.

It was your peculiar knowledge of things that were ongoing and I felt I'd be letting the side down. So I was trying to live with all this. I was dealing with the issues and then trying to juggle my own life as well. So those are the things that nobody cared about and here was no occupational health and I don't know if that was effective even when it was introduced.

In the early days it was a bottle of whiskey and keep on going. If you had success you had a bottle of whiskey, if you had a bad day you had a bottle of whiskey. That was your way of coping with the stress. If you were out and about and you were shot at, the treatment was your inspector would have brought you in and said, 'Well, young fellow, you were lucky there.' You'd throw a bottle of whiskey down your neck and then he would leave you to drive home pissed. More or less that's the way it was – that was the coping mechanism. Get a load on, go home and then get abuse from the wife for being out drinking. You were out all day working and then out all night drinking – that was police culture.

That was the turning point for me, the Cupples murder. David Cupples looked just like my son when he was there on the slab.

11:10 – Carrickmore Police Station, County Tyrone
In Carrickmore, I got a phone call one time from a wee fella who happened to work in a certain establishment in the area. He had some information relating to beer kegs going missing. This was of concern because the Provos [Provisional IRA] used the kegs to pack explosives into.

He said he had talked to his local parish priest, who had told him, 'If you think you've got information that is going to save lives you should go along to the police and tell them. But never take money for it.' So he wouldn't go to Special Branch. In his eyes that would make him a traitor or informant. So as long as he wasn't paid it was okay. Interesting little moral code.

I listened to what he had to say but I couldn't do much with the information myself. I put him on to Special Branch. They spoke to him but came back to me and said, 'Oh no, your man, he's a bit of an idiot, I wouldn't pay too much attention to him.'

Whether he was or not, I don't know. Maybe they had some other agenda. But I can tell you that a matter of days later there was another mortar attack on the station. I had been off for a couple of days over Christmas and went back. I think it was Boxing Day and he rang up again and I happened to be there doing the skeleton crew and took the call. He said to me, 'I was in a pub the other night and I heard some people talking, saying that Carrickmore's going to be mortared again within three weeks. I don't want to mention any names but I'm just letting you know.'

So off I went to Special Branch again and then to the authorities to tell them what he said. They told me it was ridiculous, that it was the same idiot, not to worry about it. I thought that I wouldn't take the risk again, so I went on the sick.

On 12 or 13 January there was a single mortar launched from across a field near the station. Four rooms were completely demolished and mine was one of them. Fortunately I wasn't there, not that anyone who could do something in the station was worried when I was trying to tell them.

The mortar contained 50lb or 100lb of explosives. By way of improving safety at the station, they had built these temporary bunkers, so the boys were in the bunkers. They weren't in the Portakabins. That was lucky because there was no protection in a Portakabin. You might as well have been in a matchbox.

11:13 – CID Office, North Belfast

Murders were happening all the time in those days from one side or the other. Just being in the wrong place at the wrong time was enough to get you killed. There was a wee man up in north Belfast, they murdered him, they put a coat over his head, just blew him away.

I remember being at the scene and two very senior officers arrived. They walked all over the crime scene. A junior constable would have known not to do that. You have to preserve the scene for the forensic team to gather any evidence.

I can still see them walking out of it and their shoes were covered in blood. The joke was, a couple of days later there were directions coming out from their office, telling you how to preserve a scene. This wee man, I never found out why he got killed. He was the caretaker up in one of the clubs in the area. A tragic, senseless murder. I don't think anybody was ever got for it either.

11:14 – Antrim Police Station

I found one of the most difficult duties to carry out was delivering death messages to people. It's a terrible job at the best of times, but when you're delivering a death message when another policeman has been murdered, it's a very unpleasant duty.

In the mid-1980s, there were these murders that became known as the Butcher Murders, because three IRA terrorists approached a police car in Newry dressed as butchers. Three police officers were shot dead. One of the policemen was called Karl Blackbourne, who was from Antrim. A young man of nineteen with his whole life ahead of him, he wasn't long in the police and wasn't even out of his probation. They even threw a hand grenade into the police car to delay the recovery of the bodies and stop first aid.

I was given the job to go and tell his parents the dreadful news. I went out to the family home and Mrs Blackbourne, she was actually away in Spain on holidays, but Mr Blackbourne was there and I pulled up and introduced myself. Where do you start? I said to him, 'Mr Blackbourne, I have some bad news.' He immediately said, 'Karl?' I said, 'Yes, it's Karl, there's been a shooting incident in Newry.' He asked, 'How bad is he? How bad is he?' I said, 'I'm so sorry, Mr Blackbourne, he's dead.' He just kept saying, 'Oh no, no, no, not Karl. What're his injuries? Will he live? He'll be okay?' I was trying to keep it together myself, and I said, 'Mr Blackbourne, listen to me. He's dead.' He just wouldn't accept it. Then he just slumped down in front of me as what I'd said sank in.

Thankfully before I'd left Antrim Station I'd made a phone call to the police doctor, Dr Stewart, and he arrived out shortly after. That was horrendous, that upset me greatly – and still does. Obviously my feelings are nothing compared to the Blackbourne family's and to Mr Blackbourne's that day. You feel so sorry for them, yet so powerless to help.

11:19 – CID Office, Belfast

You always had to keep your wits about you no matter what you were doing, particularly during the late 1970s and 1980s. The IRA were always thinking of new ways of killing police with, of course, minimum risk to themselves. This gave rise to the secondary device at incidents. You would attend a primary attack, should it be a bomb or a shooting, and think that's it over, and you start going about your investigation. That's when they catch you with the secondary device.

These attacks happened in all sorts of different circumstances and in very inventive ways. A lot of people were very fortunate in having lived to tell the tale. The golden rule was don't touch anything you don't have to. Unfortunately, human nature being what it is, coupled with a policeman's curiosity, tells you to do otherwise.

I remember a SOCO [scenes of crime officer] examining a car that had been brought into the backyard at the station. He thought there was something suspicious about it, something just not right, almost like a sixth sense. So he wouldn't go near it. We called in the ATO [army technical officer, responsible for bomb disposal] to have a look round it first. It turned out the glove compartment had been booby-trapped. It was stuffed full of explosives, and if he'd have opened it, he would have been blown to bits.

There was another one where the ATO had attended to check out an area. They cleared everything round the swimming baths as best they could, having received a report of a suspicious object in the area. One of the SOCO boys thought he saw something that looked a bit odd, out of place, so he called the ATO back out again.

The ATO came back and went to examine what the SOCO man wasn't happy with. I don't know whether he slipped or what happened to him, but when he got there the bomb went off and took the head clean off him, as neat as if you'd cut his head off with a knife. Terrible sight.

One of the boys, Sammy SOCO we called him, was out with me at a crime scene. Fortunately for those who worked with him, he was always very conscious of the risk posed by the possibility of the second device. We'd had a call about a secondary up at one of the local schools in west Belfast.

Local schools were always being broken into, but it was usually just the kids themselves breaking in. They would smash up the classrooms, spray paint, steal anything of value, just vandalism really.

We got into an army pig [heavily armoured personnel carrier] to get there, then started having a look around. I was careful because it was a school, we were doing the usual, being aware of things, looking especially for anything out of place. It's always the seemingly innocent calls that catch you.

This didn't look like the usual set-up somehow. The damage didn't look natural, more staged or something. It turned out they had booby-trapped one of the doors to a classroom. It was packed with nuts and bolts, so if we had've gone into that classroom, opening the door would have set it off and killed us.

There was a time there was another one down the country that was an ingenious one too. They were making breeze blocks and putting bombs inside the breeze blocks, sometimes just a half brick, and then sealing them. One of those was left at a policeman's house near the garage door. He came out in the morning, half-asleep I suppose, and kicked it out of the way. He was very seriously injured, lucky not to be killed.

I went to a murder at a house where a man had been shot dead. There was a radio playing in the hall when police arrived. The most natural thing in the world would have been for someone there to have said, 'Turn that bloody radio off.' Police would have been at the scene for some time but for some reason no one did. Ninety-nine times out of a hundred, someone would have turned it off. But this day it didn't happen. The radio had been packed with explosives and nails. The person turning it off would have been killed. The gunmen had left the radio in the hall on their way out.

Two policemen were killed in Donegall Pass Station in the CID office. They'd brought a shotgun in that had been found behind a shed in Benburb Street off the Donegall Road. A call had been received, reporting armed men acting suspiciously there, which turned out to be a 'come on'.

One of the men broke the shotgun open in the office and it exploded. A detective and a detective inspector were killed. Four others were seriously injured. One of them was very unlucky because it was a bit of the shrapnel from an ashtray, which was blown to smithereens in the blast, that he got hit by. It was the smallest of pieces but it cut one of his arteries and he bled to death.

All that one of the others in the office remembers is the

gun being broken open, then him just coming to, lying in the pile of rubble that used to be the office. Lessons were learnt after that. You never touch anything you aren't sure of.

11:20 – Crime Squad Office, Castlereagh Police Station, East Belfast

I have handled a number of informants over the years in the job. I wasn't Special Branch, I was CID, but I loved running informants – terrorist informants as well as ordinary criminals. One person in particular makes me think the RUC got an awful lot of bad press. But the public don't know the half of it.

There was a man I know walking about Belfast – a very, very senior Provo, heavily involved in the organisation and very close to the IRA army council at that time, Sinn Féin as well. The UVF were going to murder him: they had information about where he was going to be this day. It was a suitable and accessible location for the hit with several escape routes – they had it all sorted out.

I had an informer amongst the UVF team and, only for that informant, that boy would have been shot stone-dead. They had the murder team and all set up and ready to go. The informant was able to make contact with me by phone whilst involved with the rest of the ones and he was telling me what was happening each step of the way so that I was able to get a police vehicle to be parked close to where your man was when they arrived in the car to shoot him, scaring them off.

So, the informer actually saved that man's life and that man will never know it. There is no doubt he was a killer himself. But that's not the point. The point is that as a policeman your first duty is to protect life – all life.

11:45 – Newtownhamilton Police Station, County Armagh

This is probably one of the best attacks they had on me. After the rebuild of Crossmaglen RUC Station I went back to work at Newry for a bit, then was transferred to work at the rebuilding of Newtownhamilton RUC Station, just sticking round the border area while all this work was going on. Then I got a permanent post in the border area when everything was finished. I replaced someone who had been injured in an attack.

I was going out on my first rural patrol, a totally different way of working compared to what I was used to in Belfast. We were heading out to the border, myself and eleven soldiers. It was 12 July 1994 at 11.45 a.m. I'll never forget it. We were down in Newtownhamilton. We were ready to head out to a wee village about half a mile from the border, where they had their Orange lodges with their bands out in the street ready to have their parade.

We were going in to make sure everything was okay from a security point of view for them to have their parade locally, before they made their way to Markethill where the main parade was to be held.

We left the station to make our way there and got into position. It was more dangerous to travel by road in those days because of culvert bombs at the side of the road that would be detonated as you drove past. We would be airlifted to our patrol area if it was at all possible.

So the army sent a Puma helicopter which landed to take us out to the parade location. Where we were in Newtownhamilton, you came out of the station, crossed the road and down in to the landing pad. You always had an escort party with you to provide cover while you boarded the chopper in case of snipers because it was an open field.

We got on the chopper and the pilot, Gavin, accelerated to get us away. The next moment, we didn't know why at the time, there's a huge BOOM! It transpired a mortar bomb had been fired at us. It had either gone just over the top of us or come just underneath us but either way the blast hit the tail rotor on the helicopter.

The explosion put the back window in and the craft shifted a bit in the shockwaves. I was going, holy Moses, because we were maybe at a hundred feet by now and rising. I was going to myself, what's going on, and the next minute the Puma stuck its nose down. Then Gavin put the nose down and he started to go forwards as normal and I thought it mustn't be too bad as he was climbing at the same time. I started to feel a bit relieved.

Then I looked towards the back of the chopper. There was thick black smoke coming in through the back window. I don't know how many hundreds of feet we'd got to, but the next minute we were dropping like a stone.

The pilot had cut the engines to stop the rotation of the massive blades when we hit the ground. If you crash into the ground with them going full speed, the whole thing would just disintegrate. We were going down in a controlled descent, auto rotate they call it. I would call it hitting the ground at a right fucking rate.

What was supposed to happen with the Puma because of the size of the rotors, she was meant to put the tail down first. But we hit head first. We came down on a GAA pitch out on the Blaney Road and the rotors were digging into the ground. I was thinking at least we were on the ground. It was quite a jolt, like whiplash in a car accident. We were sitting there, trying to assess how much trouble we're in. Then I decide, yeah, that's okay, that's good.

But then I started thinking, where's the fuel tank? Because I knew we were on fire. The next thing, the craft starts to turn. I thought, that's not right, it shouldn't be happening. I was at one side of the craft and it flipped right over. I went from one side of the craft to the other and landed on another one of my patrol, a soldier. One of the guys, I could see his leg was outside and I thought he was going to lose his leg, because it was just going into the ground. Then there was this almighty scream from the gearbox. I was just waiting for the bang, and the flames, the way you would see it in the pictures. Then nothing happened.

It was eerie – everything had just stopped and everybody looked at each other in a sort of stunned silence for a few seconds. Then someone jumped up and opened the door. I was up second.

I had a Heckler & Koch MP5 machine pistol with me and just threw it out through the hatch and then I was away after it as fast as I could. When I got out I realised how badly the tail rotor was damaged. It was still on fire but it wasn't spreading so I knew the craft wasn't going to go on fire or certainly not immediately. That was a big relief too.

As we got out, the next problem we had to think about was, is a sniper about to open fire? So we had to cover the four angles around the chopper to protect each other. The soldiers were brilliant, maybe not the best unit but they were great that day. I went over to the corner, looked at this beast of a craft lying on its side, and just flumped back on to the ground, thinking to myself, how the hell did we walk away from that?

Then it was time to put the report of what had happened in by radio and get help. Remember, this was the Twelfth of July, a really busy day for the police right across the country. The main parade locally was in Markethill as I said and we were on the same radio net as there.

All I could hear on the net was that there was such and such a band going through some street, an Orange Lodge was walking up towards the assembly point and so on. I couldn't get a word in edgeways! Eventually I got a chance to get through. I transmitted through with, 'Hotel-November from Hotel-33 – contact – chopper down,' and the net just fell silent. I'll never forget it.

I radioed in that we had crashed out on the Blaney Road. We have casualities but we can look after our own, no requirement for assistance. I said we had top cover, because we had another two choppers with us. Then the boys in the station came on to say they're getting reports of serious injuries. I said, 'Look, we're okay here. Check the helipad.' Because other ones may have been injured on the ground. I didn't know where the mortar had landed.

The boys were starting to come down the road to help. When they arrived this character said to me, 'Away and have a wee break there, and sure I'll see you when you're back out again.' I says, 'Aye, dead on,' and my big mate leaned over, shook my hand and says, 'Welcome to Newtownhamilton, you lucky bastard!' No sympathy whatsoever.

I just dandered back down the road to the station on my own. I couldn't be killed as far as I was concerned at that moment, but little did I know I actually walked past the firing point, exactly where they had fired the mortar. I didn't learn that until later. They would very often be booby-trapped to kill police doing the follow-up investigation and this one was no exception. I'd walked past a bloody bomb on my way back to the station.

I arrived back into the station and my sergeant, says, 'You all right, kid?' I said, 'I'm dead on, a bit shaken up but I'll be all right.' He hands me a bottle of brandy and says, 'Get that into you.' I said, 'Right, no problem,' and went into the recreation room. I took one drink and I thought the bosses are going to be crawling all over this place shortly, and they'll come down here and see me drunk. That wasn't me, it wouldn't be professional.

All I wanted to do was talk. I phoned home, phoning my mum, my girlfriend, my mates and they were all out. It was the Twelfth of July and every single one of them was out. I couldn't get anybody to talk to. I'd have told the speaking clock about it if I could. It was just a big anti-climax. Very strange feeling.

They had reversed the mortar in on a trailer, attached to the back of a tractor. It had hay bales on it, you know the big circular ones. They had the mortar inside that, pointing out the back at an angle and had the firing system attached to an emergency generator.

They went a couple of miles outside of town and cut the power to the town off so the emergency generator kicks in just as the chopper is taking off. That fired the mortar while they were nowhere near it. It was very clever.

11:48 – CID Office, Musgrave Street Police Station, Belfast City Centre

It would have been in the early 1970s when this happened. I was attached to the CID office in Musgrave Street, Belfast. I used to go to Mass regularly with the wife. James and Susan were just youngsters at the time, but we went – unless I was working – pretty much every week as a family.

One Sunday, I saw a guy I'd gone to school with. He was a bit older than me and was with two other boys I didn't know. He was a wee shit at school. I remember when I was a kid he threw me over his shoulder, one of them judo throws, and I have a scar on my nose to this day from when I hit the ground. His name was Jimmy Doherty. He never worked in his life, he was just that used to slipping about the place. The sort of person you'd see about the town but you'd never know what he was doing there.

Then one Sunday out of the blue Jimmy Doherty came over and said, 'Hi, Matt.' I said to Jane later about Doherty,

'I've never seen him in chapel before.' She said she hadn't either. I used to get this funny feeling about these guys when I'd see them at church – might sound daft but they even seemed out of place there.

After that, the more I thought about them, the more uneasy I felt. I got Jane to go on down to the chapel separately with the children the next Sunday. I went to chapel as well, but I started taking my gun with me. I'd stay at the back rather than sit with the wife and kids. I didn't want them being in any danger because of me. You'd get a feeling that somebody was looking at you, then you start to wonder is the job getting to you and you're ending up paranoid.

Back then, I always met up every Sunday night with my mates. We would go to the club to have a few drinks and a game of snooker but this Sunday for some unknown reason I decided I didn't want go to Mass. I don't know what it was. I just wasn't comfortable about it.

Jane was a bit annoyed and started on about what sort of father and example are you when you can't go to Mass with your wife and family. But I just couldn't tell her and I remember her saying, 'If you can't go to Mass, don't be thinking you're going down to that club tonight.' That started a row.

So it came to the night and I went down to the club, saw my brothers, Billy and Tom, and we had our usual snooker, darts and drinks. It was great craic as always. I came home a bit the worse for wear. I probably stayed a bit longer than usual because of the row.

Well, it was all picture, no sound back at the house. She wasn't talking to me because I had defied her and went to the club. All through Monday was the same. Tuesday morning I was glad to head off to work to get a bit of peace.

I went into the office and after a while of course the

chief calls me into his office to have a word with me. I was unconcerned. I thought I'm just transferred down here from Springfield Road CID Office. I was still a detective and I was very keen and taking as many cases as I could to get myself through probation.

He got me to sit down and he said, 'I want to talk to you about the weekend. Did you go to Mass on Sunday?' I thought, 'Holy shit, don't tell me the wife's called the fucking chief because I didn't go to Mass.' I said, 'No, chief, I didn't.'

He said, 'Do you know a Doherty?' Of course I thought of all the criminals in our local patch in Belfast. Then he said, 'Jimmy Doherty from Bangor.' I said, 'If it's the Jimmy Doherty I'm thinking of, I went to school with him.' 'And you didn't go to Mass on Sunday?' I was thinking, 'Where's this going?' I said, 'No, chief, I didn't.' He just came over and put his arm round my shoulder. 'I can tell you now, Matt, if you had gone to Mass on Sunday, you wouldn't be sitting here today. You'd be a dead man.' I was shocked and just said, 'What?', trying to take in what I was hearing.

Doherty was sent down to Bangor because he knew me to see and the hit team had come down too. When he was saying hello to me that particular Sunday at the chapel, he was confirming who the target was – identifying me to the trigger man who was planning to murder me.

Some stuff I have only actually found out in this last year or two was that there was an AK-47 assault rifle to be used and the gunman was absolutely livid whenever they had risked the journey with guns to Bangor that the spotters couldn't see me.

When they got back to the safe house in Belfast for their debrief he was still livid. The very fact that something had happened to cause me not to be there – where was I? He sent them back again to look for me.

They didn't get me anyway, but I found out later there was a witch-hunt internally in the IRA, because obviously they felt there was a tout [police informant] on the go. They reckoned somebody had warned me or in reality their handlers and that was why I wasn't there that Sunday. They felt it was your man [names person] who then had a house on the Belfast Road, who did a disappearing act and to this day he has never been found back here again. So I think he actually was a tout, but he's not why I didn't go. Though obviously the chief didn't get all the detailed information he had from me.

Doherty and his accomplice McShane had joined the IRA about a year before that and they had set me up, for what reason I'll never know – just a Catholic policeman, I suppose, and an easy target for them. They had plans to kill another Catholic policeman in Bangor as well. Why somebody in the police didn't tell me, I don't know. Maybe I was going to be used to protect a tout. You'll never get that answer, of course, they'll never tell you. The assistant chief constable did tell me, though, that there was no way they would ever compromise a policeman to protect a source.

Doherty's brother was very friendly with me. We always used to get on very well together. But from that day to this, anytime he sees me he always puts his head down or walks on the other side of the road. I was in court and they all got prison for conspiracy to murder me. Doherty's dad was a barman for a long time in Fealty's. The father, he was a decent man. They were a very republican family and looked on me as a traitor; a traitor for going into the RUC. A lot of Englishmen also found it hard to believe that you're a Catholic in the RUC. The IRA were quicker to murder Catholic officers to scare others off joining but that gets happily ignored.

12:05 – Unit Beat, Divis Flats, West Belfast

The unit beat was really started because the authorities wanted to show that the police could get back out on to the streets in all parts of Belfast and that there weren't any no-go areas. We had to have so many soldiers with us to ensure the safety of the police on the ground. We used to go out in a brick formation, which is an army technical term for their patrols. The hope was to try and reach out to the people. There were a lot of kids playing around the flats. So we tried to get community relations going a bit between them and the police so they could realise we weren't the monsters perhaps we had been painted to be.

The kids used to talk away to us. One girl particularly was very friendly and chatty. She was a very young girl, but over the weeks and months you get to know them and they get to know you. It's just an evolving relationship. She was a very sharp wee girl and she used to give me information.

She would spot things around the area, which a child maybe would normally have to be older to have noticed. She would see things around the balconies and the alleyways of the flats, which are tall and a bit of a maze. She would pass the information on in an innocent sort of a way, I suppose.

She would notice Provos speaking together and being about the area. She would say things like, 'I saw them at the third balcony along, the second door. There were men going in and out all evening.' Things that were irregular. She would spot it because everyone knew each other, so strangers stuck out. Her being a kid, they took no notice of her. She probably inadvertently saved a number of lives with just simple pieces of information which may have fitted with what we knew already.

The family themselves weren't the best. They had a dark history with drink, drugs and indeed sexual abuse within the family. It was ongoing and you got to know that it was fairly rife within the area. She had a hard life through her early years.

One day she arrived down into Hastings Street Police Station in a terrible state. She went into the enquiry office and told the guy at the desk, 'I must speak to Sergeant Tim. It has to be Sergeant Tim.' Eventually the fella got hold of me. She was able to tell me about a bomb that was planted in the flats, which was a booby trap to try and murder myself and my colleagues when we were on foot patrol.

She had overheard them talking about it, the IRA, and saw where exactly they were placing it. She had seen the bomb being brought out. She saw everything that was going on and passed it on to me. So apart from anything else that may have happened, I have to say that I and some of my colleagues unquestionably owe her our lives.

I used to help her out as best I could. I have daughters myself, and as they grew out of clothes, I used to get them to her and would just give her a hand to try and improve her prospects in life. She was trying to get out of this terrible rut she had been in with the family. She was always very keen to break the cycle and get a family of her own and get away, I suppose.

She had been very strong the way she'd managed to improve herself. She got clean of any drink or drugs problems. She worked hard to cut ties with the family and actually got qualified to work in social services helping others. Then when she wanted to get married – of course she had no dad to speak of – she actually asked me if I would give her away. I was very honoured and I actually postponed taking the Patten redundancy offer to do so because I had intended moving away from Northern Ireland.

She's a lovely girl and she has kids of her own now and indeed grandchildren. She's been a great mother. She's very happily married and she moved away and has made something of herself. So it is possible to do it from the worst of circumstances. I am very proud of her that she managed to do it. We are in touch to this day and any time when I'm back in the Province, we would always meet up. She is a super girl and a credit to herself. I'm proud to have played a part in her life.

12:16 – CID Office, Antrim Road Police Station, North Belfast

I was sitting in Antrim Road Station with Tony Johnston, who was my detective inspector at the time. We got a report of a shooting in the Diamond Jubilee Bar on the Shankill Road. He and I headed across to it and when we got there we found a guy called Harry Ward had been shot dead.

He had been in the bar when two gunmen from the IPLO [Irish People's Liberation Organisation] had walked in looking for a top loyalist named Bunter Graham. They even shouted, 'Where's Bunter? Where's Bunter?' He wasn't there. But they saw Ward, who they thought looked a bit like him. He ran through the bar into the off-sales to try and get away from them. He had spotted them coming towards the bar. But they went in after him and shot him dead. His running may have confirmed the mistaken identification by the gunmen. Four other people who were also in the bar were unharmed.

We arrived at the scene, the uniform police had it cordoned off. All the locals were starting to appear and a crowd was gathering outside. We were going about our business, trying to get things sealed off inside to preserve the scene. The next thing, Johnny Adair, who was a well-known senior terrorist on the loyalist side, arrived. He had with him his usual cronies. As others arrived at the scene, you could see them talking amongst themselves. It was soon obvious that an extremely heated conversation was going on.

I said to Tony Johnston, 'We need to try to get surveillance on them. Those boys are going to go out tonight and shoot somebody.' I just knew the way they were talking that they were scheming. We dealt with the whole thing at the bar in the meantime, knowing full well that the next scene we would be attending was being planned just feet away.

It's easy to say, 'Get surveillance,' but it's not that simple in practical terms. You can't deploy just like that and it didn't happen to my knowledge. Later that day, when we were having our tea up in Antrim Road again, a call came in to say a taxi driver had been shot dead down in Rosapenna Street. Off I went again to scene number two, another murder. It was a week after my mother had died. This was my first day back at work after burying my mother. The taxi driver had been coming out on to the Oldpark Road, just at the junction. Loyalist paramilitary gunmen came up on foot and shot him in the head. His passengers were uninjured. A decent man, not involved in anything. What I had feared turned into reality. I had to deal with my second murder that day, which I knew was connected to the first but I was powerless to prevent it.

12:23 – Belfast Magistrates Court

A guy I dealt with did a break-in and stole a guitar. It was Chinese New Year and they were celebrating when they heard a window being broken up around Howard Street. They came out of their place and saw someone make off with a guitar under his arm. From the description that was given I had an idea who this thief might be. In those days you got to know your local criminals.

I decided to search his place. I found him, the guitar and, as a bonus, not only was there blood on the guitar, he also had cuts on his fingers and hands from the window that had been broken. Plus there was blood on the window. I arrested him, brought him into the police office in Townhall Street from where you would appear in court the next day.

The Magistrates Court was always a bit of a madhouse but I was just looking for an adjournment. You could have turned round to the magistrate and said you believed he was going to commit further offences. You could request putting him into custody until you'd finished getting your paperwork together. I remember the Chinese guy was there to give evidence. He had identified the burglar running away. He wanted a saucer brought into court and the saucer was then broken. He said, 'If I tell a lie, may my soul be broken like this saucer.' It was their way of being sworn in.

Then the solicitor started putting up the defence for him. I got called to start giving evidence, but I didn't want the case to go ahead because I'd had the blood and the guitar dusted for fingerprints and samples to check the blood, but I hadn't got any evidence as such. So I wanted to get it adjourned, which would be normal at this stage.

The magistrate said to the defending solicitor, 'Look, Detective Constable Davidson is always in this court and he's never failed yet. He always tells the truth. I don't see any reason why I shouldn't believe him now. I'm finding him guilty. Constable Davidson has said that he found blood and got the blood analysed.' I hadn't said that, I hadn't even started the case.

The solicitor went to protest again and he just told him to sit down or he would hold him in contempt of court. He just sat down and your man was convicted. I hadn't even put pen to paper, let alone got a case together.

13:09 – Shankill Bomb, Shankill Road, West Belfast

I dealt with what became known locally as the 'Shankill Bomb' at Frizzell's fish shop on the Shankill Road. I was sitting in Antrim Road Station, having my lunch, chatting with a few other peelers when I heard the explosion. It was a pretty big explosion. My immediate thought was this doesn't sound too good. The phone rang. It was my boss. 'We need everybody across to the Shankill to the scene.'

Billy Kildea was the detective inspector in charge of the investigation, I was the detective sergeant. We dealt with all we could at the scene, what a hell of a scene it was. Total carnage with bodies and bits of bodies everywhere. Nine people were murdered in the explosion. Innocent Saturday afternoon shoppers. A further fifty-seven people were injured, including one of the bombers. A tenth person died, but he was a bomber carrying the device into the premises. Four women and two children were amongst the dead.

Part of my job was to try and coordinate vaguely everything that happened, to try and get it into some sort of order. We had reports coming in that one of the bombers who was in a white coat had arrived at the Mater Hospital with multiple injuries and my job was to go over, get the clothing and try and get all the evidence I could find tied down initially.

I must say the staff at the Mater Hospital were superb. They had the presence of mind to preserve the white coat that Sean Kelly was wearing and that was to prove crucial down the line in the investigation. They weren't happy with him when he came in, they smelt a rat immediately. Once he was arrested, he was then moved to Musgrave Park Hospital, where there was a secure wing that he could be detained in.

My next job was to go with Billy and meet all the families of the deceased. Then we had to try to rebuild the whole scene again: where people were on the Shankill Road on the Saturday. You can imagine the number of people there were that we had to try and place at the scene. The task was to try and reconstruct the scene in the shop before the explosion and establish exactly where everyone was. We knew there was probably more than the two bombers we knew about at this stage involved.

It was amazing to see the reconstruction of the actual fish shop built up. One of the things I had to do every day in the process had a lot to do with clothing. I had to keep looking at the post-mortem photographs of the kids. You were trying to compare clothing and the description of people from the relatives.

You like to think photographs don't have an impact on you, but actually, over a period of time, they do. Especially when you've attended the scene of what they are showing yourself. Forensics rebuilt the counter and the wall out of skip-loads of rubble that had been removed when the building had been knocked down.

We were actually able to reconstruct the very counter where the device was placed by the bomber. It sat in the forensic lab for years. I don't know where it is now and actually the forensic guy was able to rebuild part of the bomb, the timing device that was recovered from the rubble. When you think about the tons and tons of rubble – unbelievable.

We went to interview Kelly, one of the bombers, in the hospital. We had pre-determined questions written out, as we knew the bastard probably wouldn't speak to us. But we went anyway to go through the formality of putting the questions about the bombing to him. His solicitor sat outside and looked through the window. We went through the process of a normal interview, cautioned him and then we fired a series of questions at him and the whole time that we were questioning him he had rosary beads in his hands and he was rubbing them. He wouldn't answer at all, just wouldn't speak.

His face was all speckled with the injuries from the blast. He looked like a fifteen-year-old boy lying there – frightening, to be truthful. At the end of it all, I said to him, 'You can rub all you want at your rosary beads, because you're going to have a long time to spend with them. The rest of your life will be spent in prison.' And I walked out.

We had managed to gather quite a pile of evidence against him and I thought we had built a very strong case. It eventually went to court. He pleaded not guilty, but he didn't get cross-examined as a witness as he opted not to give evidence on his own behalf.

He didn't recognise the court. He was to get life in prison and I think he served perhaps seven years. He got out under the Good Friday Agreement. He's back at it again and that really annoys me. There's a guy, put away for life, kills nine innocent people and he's running the streets and he's still involved. I've done all I can do, but the law said let him out again. If I feel like that, how do some of the injured parties or the victims feel? I know some of them have taken it on board and accepted it. But I know if it was me, I couldn't.

Incidentally the getaway driver [names person], he was a real hero, he took off shortly after the explosion. The Provos sent him down south for a number of weeks to get his story right. They even went through mock interviews for days with him before he was allowed to come back north. They must have thought he wouldn't hold up too well during interview if we'd got him earlier.

13:11 – Castlereagh Holding Centre, East Belfast
When I first went into CID I can remember my feeling of

excitement when I was told I was going over to Castlereagh Holding Centre to interview someone for the first time. It seemed a major step up along the path of my time in the police. I'd heard so much about the place but I'd never really been in it. In we went to find out who we would be interviewing and I'm looking all round me but pretending I'm not. I had a very experienced detective with me. He became a very close friend over the years. We started off by getting an intelligence briefing from the other detectives as to how the person you are going to be speaking to has been behaving. Some of them speak, some of them don't. Some lie on the floor, they undress, they urinate in the interview room. I even know of one IRA man who started to masturbate during interview in front of a policewoman. Anyway we got the brief about how this fellow had been and apparently he had been very cocky and cheeky since he had arrived.

The detective with me said, 'I don't like this bastard and I haven't met him yet.'

We went to get him out of the cell to have him brought upstairs to the interview room. We were escorted upstairs with him by a uniform officer, which was standard practice. Sure enough he had a really cocky walk, he was quite a senior terrorist. He swaggered along to show us nothing was any bother to him. He walked very slowly as if he was in charge of everything and hadn't a care in the world.

In the interview room, he sat his backside in the chair and the detective with me just walked in and hit him with an open-handed slap in the face. This lifted him straight off the seat, sending him crashing against the wall. He then went over to him and picked him up by the cheeks of his face and put him back in the chair. He put one foot either side of him, while he sat on the table, and said, 'I'm gonna ask you questions and when I ask them, you answer me yes, no, I don't know. You tell me the truth, and if you don't, I'm going to reintroduce myself.'

He gave him the rounds of the kitchen for the next four hours, and the cockiness was gone. For years afterwards, I joked with him that I was nearly ready to say I did it.

14:15 – Uniform Patrol, Blacks Road, West Belfast

The Twelfth of July was on the Sunday that year, so the parade was going to be a day later on the Monday. We were sitting down at Blacks Road. It was the interface for a small Prod area beside a large nationalist one. The bands were heading down to the field to join up with the main demonstration doing the parade. There were police and army all round, keeping an eye on things.

We were sitting with the doors open, because it was a nice sunny morning. And because we were in a Prod area, we felt that wee bit safer. Three of us were in the armoured car. The next thing, bullets started flying. You knew it was an AK-47. You could actually tell by the report from the gun. The next minute, the doors closed, engine on and we moved forward, waiting for word coming through on the radio of what was happening. There was a guy standing at the bus stop beside us waving madly at us and pointing at a car that was going past.

It was a mustard-coloured Lada Estate, I'll never forget it. As it drove past you could actually see the three gunmen in the car. You could see their eyes. We moved off in the car and fell in behind the Lada. I was only in my first six months of police service, so my local knowledge wasn't great.

We were driving down Blacks Road, tucked in behind the car the gunmen were in. The next minute, the back-seat passenger was hanging out behind the driver through the window. The front-seat passenger was hanging out the other side of the car. They just started hammering us with the AKs. I'll tell you, we were in an armoured car, but we were under a hail of automatic gunfire. It was like something out of a Bruce Willis film.

I was trying to make myself smaller. There was nothing we could do except try and keep going after them, radioing in where they were. We couldn't return fire because we were in a bulletproof car and the windows didn't go down. Every time there was a strike on the windscreen, my head was going down even though the glass was armoured. Your head might tell you it's okay – but your bowels don't seem to get the message when the lead's flying.

They ended up killing the engine of our car. They shot the engine to bits which shows you the number of rounds that were being fired at us. We chased them as fast as we thought we could go, then the car would hardly move. I didn't think they could do that to the engine but they were able to. We started to limp back to the station as best we could to get her going again.

The barricades were up everywhere around the area. There was also petrol bombs being thrown at nearly every junction, mixed with widespread rioting on the arterial routes throughout the area. The speed with which republicans could orchestrate a riot would amaze you. This was all to help the gunmen get away and prevent follow-up action by the police. We came up out of Riverdale up on the Andersonstown Road and where we came out was between all the barricades. We were in trouble, and our car not going too well didn't help.

The police Land Rovers were piling in as well, to try and get us back out again. If we were trapped in the crowd of rioters, we were dead, simple as that. Eventually they cleared us a bit of a path and we tried to get up to Woodburn Station again.

As we got there, one of the army pigs was coming out of

the gate. We stopped to let them pass, at which point the car conked out completely. The pig came on forward and smacked straight into us. Those things must weigh about eight tons, so any forensics at the front of the car from the shooting were ruined.

When we got the car inside the station I opened the door to get out and a bullet dropped down from where it had lodged in the side at the door – the gunmen were shooting at us before we got the doors closed and made the turn to go after them.

That was fairly scary, too, knowing how close it was. But, as usual, you only realise afterwards. If they had been armour-piercing rounds, they would have been straight through that windscreen and I wouldn't be telling you about what happened.

14:18 – Crumlin Road, North Belfast

I'd just left the CID office at Tennent Street and was driving down the Crumlin Road. I saw a crowd of people running across the road in front of me.

It turned out that I had just stumbled across an IRA shooting of a sergeant stationed at Tennent Street, Danny O'Connor, and a guy who I didn't know. They had both been walking down the Crumlin Road on their way to escort an Orange parade. Both of them had been shot when a white Morris 1100 car came out of Clifton Park Avenue and sprayed the footpath, hitting Danny in the chest and his colleague in the legs. They didn't stand a chance.

An ambulance was sent for and I went with the both of them to hospital in the back of it. Danny O'Connor died in my arms in the ambulance, which really brought it home to me as to how savage the place was. Ultimately an ex-internee was convicted and got ten years – an IRA man from Ardoyne. Another ex-internee was charged but the charges were later dropped. It was the second time he had been cleared on a murder charge. The Crumlin Road had been busy with shoppers so any police in the area were unable to return fire.

14:20 – Uniform Police, Downpatrick Police Station

In Downpatrick, when I was in uniform, we used to go out in the summertime to Tyrella to do a patrol of the beach to look at the talent. Not that there was that much to look at, but on a good day it got very busy and there were lots of ladies about.

We were paying that much attention to the girls in their swimsuits we forgot about the tide. We actually got stuck in the sand. We got a call-out to come back in to get cattle off the road somewhere. We were going nowhere. I had to tell them that we were otherwise engaged without details and hope for the best.

Meanwhile, my partner had gone to the local farmer and asked if we could get a tow out of the mess we were in. This is in front of the whole of the beach, which was bunged. The police car had to be towed out and nobody ever knew we were there, because it wasn't even our police area. Embarrassing to say the least – thankfully there weren't as many cameras around in those days, and we didn't end up on the front page of the local paper.

14:27 – CID Office, Antrim Road Police Station, North Belfast

In one of the other cases that always sticks with me, Bogie was the culprit. Bogie was a great detective but could never get used to the fact that the interviews were being taped. He was used to the old-fashioned way when you wrote the notes, but he had vast experience.

We arrested a boy for rape (it actually turned out he murdered Daphne Taylor, a retired schoolteacher in Bangor, while she was out walking her dog along the coastal path). He was ex-French Foreign Legion. I had arrested him for questioning as a suspect. I was investigating a case where a sixteen-year-old girl was raped in a garden up the Antrim Road.

We eventually tracked him down and got him in for questioning. There were 110 typed pages of interview notes which, believe me, is a lot of notes and an indication of how difficult the interview had been. I had to read every word of them out in open court in front of a jury. It was an awful job. It was like reading them a novel. Every third word was 'fuck'. It was Bogie doing all the swearing.

He had pleaded not guilty to all the charges so the case was being contested. The judge actually stopped me halfway through reading the interview notes to ask, 'Sergeant, would you like a drink?' meaning water, obviously. This was the way it went on the whole way through. It didn't matter to Bogie, he had just kept going. He couldn't get his head round the fact that this was going to be recorded and, of course, he didn't have to get into the witness box and read it out, it was me. I could actually feel the jury looking at me at times thinking, this is a police officer saying this. It was a total nightmare!

Richard Close was the rapist's name. He's out now. If I saw him now I might not know him, but he'll remember me and that's always the case when you've been in Castlereagh. You meet that many, you can't remember all of them. But rest assured they will remember you, and that's the danger. He made threats to me during interview.

He was a bad boy, very cocky and that's what let him down, his arrogance. A wee sixteen-year-old-girl, a random attack.

In fact, he was arrested following a random attack on a female in Castle Park in Bangor, directly across the road from his granny's house in Abbey Street, where he was to reside while on bail. He attacked this female who was walking through the park. It was a vicious attack but she fought back. The female was grabbed from behind. As he smashed the victim's head into the ground, her screams were heard by her teenage son and his friend who lived nearby. They grabbed a spade and managed to fend Close off. The boys watched the direction Close took off in and called the police. He was subsequently arrested at his granny's house. No doubt they saved the victim from certain death.

When he was charged with the murder of Daphne Taylor, I got a phone call from the superintendent and he says, 'Andy, why did this guy get bail?' I said, 'Good question, boss. I opposed it on every occasion.' They were looking to hang me out to dry over the murder.

I was going over to see the superintendent for a bollocking because of what happened, but thankfully on every occasion that I had been up on the bail hearing, I had opposed bail for the simple reason that it was a random attack. It's annoying when you are doing your best, doing what you can to help people in general and you've got to watch your back because of people in authority, your own bosses, people who you know well are just waiting on the slightest slip. They were looking for a scapegoat and would have happily sold me down the river to protect themselves.

One of the things that you learn when you're doing SIO [senior investigating officer] work is that you fill in your policy book religiously. Your policy book is really what, on a daily basis, you have been doing during the investigations – a record of the decisions you are making and why.

A generation before me, they didn't have the accountability there is now. Even in my early days there wasn't the same accountability. But in the latter years, you had to watch every stroke of the pen. You hear all this crap about collusion, I have never ever been involved. I just think it's nonsense but I'm not saying there may not have been individual cases. But in over thirty-one years I never even saw or heard a hint of it.

14:31 – Surveillance Duty, Greater Belfast Area

I was out one day in Belfast in a surveillance van with my sergeant. We were listening to the local radio net for the uniform police attending calls. We would always have had the local radio channel on so that we didn't stumble into anything by accident. This day we heard the initial report that there'd been a shooting in the area we were in. A young guy had been shot dead.

The Provisional IRA had claimed the murder by telephone, giving a recognised code word – once the terrorists involved had made good their escape and got back to the safe house to clean up and burn their clothes to destroy any forensic evidence.

When the IRA claimed the killing, they said the person they had murdered was a serving police officer. The police attending the scene weren't able to confirm this. He had no identification on him and none of the police present recognised him.

My sergeant and I parked the van near where it happened and went over to the scene to see if we could help identify the body. The person, who would have been in his twenties, had been shot three times in the face. He didn't stand a chance. The scene had obviously been examined, but the body hadn't been removed yet. He was lying as he fell. The uniformed personnel pulled the sheet back so that I could see his face. But I didn't recognise him. I can see his face now as I'm telling this.

I left them to it and we went back to what we were doing. Later on that day, I got a phone call from an inspector in Special Branch that I knew, asking me if I'd heard about the shooting in Belfast that morning. I said, 'Yes, as a matter of fact, I was out and about at the time and went down to the scene to see if I could help identify the victim.'

He asked me then did I notice his car and I said, 'No, I didn't.' Well, it so happened the victim had the same type of car as me and the registration number only varied on one digit. He lived behind the police station I was operating out of at the time.

It transpired the targeting of the victim had gone wrong when the IRA started to look into planning the murder, following him, getting to know his movements to work out the best place to kill him. He was unfortunately shot dead but I was the intended victim.

That made me a member of a very unique sort of club, in that I've attended my own murder. It's a very strange feeling and I know I tend to make light of it, because I don't know how else to deal with it. I think of that day and picture what I saw more often than I care to admit.

Obviously I had to take steps to up my personal security to say the least. I started by going to get some false plates, security plates as they're called, and put them on to the car. It means the IRA can't use their contacts in the Vehicle Licensing Authority to find out the owner's name and address. I had to sell the car immediately. Then you have to get through to friends and family to be conscious of their security. They just don't understand how a careless word or joke in the wrong place can be overheard and be potentially lethal.

It was a harrowing experience and one of those things in life that makes you stop and think.

14:45 – Uniform Patrol, Shaws Road, West Belfast

I was in Woodburn in west Belfast. It was my first station after I passed out of the training centre in early 1981. It was the time of the hunger strikes at the Maze Prison. They had started near enough as soon as I arrived. There was a lot of street disorder in the area and attempts by terrorists to kill police were relatively common. It was a tense time.

We were called to a suspect vehicle up on the Shaws Road. We headed up in convoy to see what the score was. A Land Rover was placed on either side of the road to block the traffic, because you could tell the lorry had been abandoned deliberately. There were two police Land Rovers and an army Land Rover in the patrol, which was normal. So we had the army Land Rover positioned up above the lorry, we were down below, I was in the back, I was the rear gunner. We had the sergeant out with us – he was in the front, Big Gary was driving. There were five of us in total in the truck.

The inspector arrives and goes straight over to the abandoned lorry, looks into the back of it, looks into the cab, under and around it, then he waves us up towards it. But just before we went up, we had been chatting away amongst ourselves because it was quarter to three and we finished at three o'clock.

Everybody was just wanting to get out of there. We wanted to get this lorry off the road and get away home. We knew if we called the army out with the bomb disposal boys we would be there for hours.

Gary said, 'I can drive that thing, I've done it before. Let's get the road cleared and get away home. I'll move it.' The sergeant actually turned around and said to Gary, 'You'll do that once too often.' Gary said, 'Look, I've got my HGV. I'll drive this back to the station.' We all got out and the five of us walked to the front of the lorry.

The inspector had moved back up the road a bit. Gary — huge big guy — he would have been my senior man. He was like my tutor. He would be looking after me any time I was doing observer. He kept me right with the paperwork and what to do.

Something said to me inside, no grouping, just something was telling me no grouping. I walked round to the back of the lorry. I had the machine gun as well, so I was giving cover to the rest of the guys who were out on the ground. I was looking into Lenadoon for anything out of place and bang, the bloody lorry went up.

I looked up to see the cab coming down out of the air. I was shaking from the blast at the back of the lorry. I didn't know what had happened. Was Gary in it? Was it a rocket attack? Would there be a secondary explosion?

Gary had climbed inside the cab. He had taken the full blast, he had actually saved the rest of the boys from taking very serious injuries. The sergeant was badly burned. The Brit, Alan, an ex-squaddie, he was badly burned too. He never really returned after that. One of the guys up the other side, he got hit by a bit of shrapnel in the leg, a wee reserve man. As soon as I looked up and saw the roof of the cab coming down, I just ran to the other Land Rover up above. Bodies were strewn all over the place. Other boys came, the Blues [local DMSU patrol] arrived. Because of everything that was happening, I was still trying to get cover, because you didn't know whether there was another one.

I had actually cocked the gun, and was pointing into this estate. There were kids and everything about the place. I could hear somebody shouting, 'God's sake, mind the kids.'

I was still only eighteen years of age. I was shit-scared, but the more people arrived, the calmer I got because I knew I had help. It was an absolute nightmare. Gary was in the back of the ambulance with the sergeant. He saw me and he literally sat up in the back of the ambulance to say cheerio when he just died. He had massive internal injuries.

It was a mercury tilt-switch detonator device under the seat. With Gary being so big, it didn't even wait until he moved the lorry before it exploded. I went home and my mum met me at the door and I couldn't say anything. I just went straight up the stairs, crying.

I went down to see my uncle Jack. He had been in the job for twenty-odd years. I went to see him because I knew he would understand. There's no one you can talk to, you can't put your family through it. Other cops get it and understand where you're coming from. Normal people don't.

I was told just take as long as you want off work. The next morning, I said to myself, if I don't go back in today I'll never go back. So I phoned them up because I had no car and someone came out, picked me up and drove me in to the station. Just as we were driving back in, there was a bomb scare in the front of the station. In Woodburn, it was just one incident after another.

14:57 – Coffee Break

Another thing I found very hard to deal with was anything involving children. I can remember going to a fatal road traffic accident in Ballycastle. It was a wee girl of ten. I forget her name now, because it was so many years ago. She had been out riding her bicycle on this country road and this car came along and hit her.

I went to the scene when it happened, but revisiting the scene the next day, you could still tell. She had been wearing a red woollen cardigan. When I got to the scene the next day to see if I missed anything, I could still see the bits of fluff along the tarmac on the road. I carry that in my mind to this day.

Don't get me wrong, I was very privileged to have been a police officer, to serve a community totally, impartially. I met some great friends within the police service and I met some fantastic people who I had to deal with in the course of my duties. But I have paid quite a horrendous price for it. Because, unfortunately, I took to heavy drinking near the end of my service.

I seemed to be able to cope with everything all right up until I retired. Then I started to have these dreams and nightmares about things that happened over the years. They were recurring and I was drinking heavier and heavier until I became an alcoholic. Thank God, I rang a friend, and I went to AA. I've been sober now twelve years in December. My first day without a drink was 8 December 2004. I take it just a day at a time but the dreams continue and they are horrific.

There was one just three nights ago. I woke up in the morning, my pyjama top was just wringing with sweat. In the dream I had just been through a hell of a horrific gunfight in Derry. I don't know what brings it on, but I would have those sort of dreams at least three to four times a week. Every night I am deprived of my sleep. I awaken in the morning, I'm exhausted to the extent that I have to go to bed sometimes in the afternoon.

That is something I have to live with. Would I do it again? I don't know. I know people paid more, people paid the ultimate price. There were colleagues of mine who paid with their lives. But it is also affecting me emotionally because I find it very difficult to watch anything where there is any sadness in it or violence.

I cannot watch programmes concerning Northern Ireland. I cannot watch violent programmes, even if they are fictitious. I can't control my emotions, my dreams and nightmares. I would wish it on no one.

That said I am proud of what I did. I was proud to be a member of the RUC. It's now the PSNI and God love those young men and women. I wish them well, but I only hope that they have the integrity that all members of the RUC that I ever came into contact with had. They stood proud of their title, proud of their job, proud of the role that they played in society, proud of what they contributed to the peace process.

The peace process wasn't only brought about by politicians. The RUC paid a very heavy price. I've paid a heavy price, my children have paid a heavy price, my wife has paid a heavy price and I continue to pay. But I am proud of what I did and very proud of all my colleagues.

Lates
15:00–23:00 hours

15:01 – Newry Police Station

I went to Newry in 1992, I think it was. This was just after the horizontal mortar attack when a policewoman was killed and her colleague lost his leg. Newry had to be one of the worst places on this earth for policemen. That place was scarier than Ballymurphy, which I always considered to be one of the worst places. But in Newry, if I was going out on a patrol, especially at night, I didn't know if I was coming back. The people I worked with there would do anything for each other. That's how good the comradeship was. It was so tight.

Hallowe'en – you knew that a few of the men would be messing about in the locker rooms with fireworks. You would wait until somebody was half-dressed and then throw a firework when they couldn't do anything about it. But down there you couldn't take a chance and dismiss the explosion as a prank. They couldn't move because their trousers were down round their ankles. And of course the thing goes bang. Some very funny sights came hopping out of those locker rooms.

In Newry I was always wandering around with an earpiece for the radio stuck in my head because you just didn't know what was going to happen or when. I heard a loud boom one day. I asked, 'What was that? Was that just somebody letting a firework off out the front?' Then a garbled message came through on the radio and I knew for sure something had happened out the front of the station.

I was first out. There were two security gates, and one had to close before the other opened. So the guy in the sanger [reinforced security post] couldn't get out to them because he was the one in control of the gates. He couldn't release the gate, so he let me out the side [emergency exit]. I went running out and I was just at the road and I could see immediately that Woodsie was down. The street hadn't been cleared – meaning I couldn't go up it – so I was just going to let off a couple of rounds. There was a Land Rover across the road and an armoured car sitting beside it. I went across and the other guy was cowering in the corner, holding on to an MP5 machine gun. A sniper had hit Woodsie, shot him through the throat.

Woodsie was in my section at the station. We were actually working overtime with the late crew. We had just changed shifts. I was saying, 'You're going to be all right,' over and over, trying to reassure him. Another guy, Davey, came running out. We put a bandage on his neck to stem the blood, but he just kept looking straight up into the air. He wasn't moving or anything. I was holding his hand just telling him he was going to be all right.

Everybody was crashing out to help. The cars were screaming in from the country to try and get the place cleared. An ambulance had been called. The DMSU were crashing out of Downshire Road. Everything seemed to me to be taking forever. There was still no ambulance and I was shouting to the skipper, 'Colin, he's gonna die here if we don't move him.'

I said, 'Get that car started.' But the battery was dead because it had been sitting at the front of the station for ages. At last the ambulance arrived. It probably was only a couple of minutes but it seemed like an eternity. The ambulance lifted him. As the paramedics were working on his injuries, I picked up the MP5 that the other guy, Rod, had been holding. I cocked the gun and the round came out. Even in his panic, he'd still made the gun ready to fire. It was good what he had done. Then it was just case of me using it to give cover while the ambulance guys were doing what they do. Woodsie was in Daisy Hill Hospital in Newry for a wee while and then transferred to Craigavon Area Hospital. Sadly, he died two days later, but he was probably one of the ones who had survived the sniper the longest.

The round that sniper used would go through the engine block, through the car, through the flak jacket, there's no answer to it. They had these plates in the body armour to wear at the permanent vehicle checkpoints during the rebuild of Crossmaglen Station. They were like porcelain. You'd think if you dropped them, they'd smash. But apparently they stopped the round. But if it was wrapped round you, it might push one plate on to the other plate which would probably stop your heart anyway. So unless you had somebody there that was going to be able to start your heart again, why would you even bother wearing the thing?

Woodsie was just about to move into his new home: he had just built this big fuck-off house for his wife and daughter. His wee daughter took her first steps in the hospital. It was so sad. I think he realised how bad he was. They took the life support machine off. He was going to be a paraplegic anyway. The round had severed his spine. That was a nightmare. That was Newry for you.

Things had been mounting up at that time because we had been trying to get these permanent solid walls built to stop all this shooting at the station. That sniper was causing havoc in the area. After Woodsie was killed, they spent the money, they put the barricades up. But it was too late.

15:02 – Rural Patrol, County Down

Another story that has always amused me happened away down the country. There was a sergeant I had. He was a good man and a very experienced policeman who knew the area like the back of his hand. There was a constant problem with gypsies in the area. The responsibility to keep crime down ultimately rested with the local sergeant, and try as he might he just couldn't get through to them. They were just one big nuisance. They were always up to something – thieving and stealing and operating some scam or other. His heart was broken with them.

He went out and he talked to them regularly but of course they knew nothing about anything. In fact half the time you didn't even know the real identity of the person you were standing talking to. The sergeant went out to the camp this day and it was the usual story. He was at the end of his tether, totally exasperated. They had this old dog running about the site and the sergeant said to them, 'Is that dog licensed?' They said, 'That dog's nothing to do with us; it's not our dog.' The sergeant turned, looked across, drew his gun and shot the dog dead on the spot. Now he had their full attention. He then looked at one of the men and then he looked across the site and he said, 'Is that your donkey over there?' The man said, 'Ah now, sergeant, not the donkey. If you give us half an hour we'll be out of here.' He thought for sure the donkey was going to be next.

15:03 – CID Office, Queen Street Police Station, Belfast City Centre

I got this call one day. A wee lad, only thirteen, had been raped. Jimmy and I investigated the case. He was raped in the underground toilet across from the City Hall. He was waiting on his mum to pick him up and went down to have a wee and this bastard pulled him into the cubicle and raped him. He had marks all around the back of his neck where the man had sucked and bit into him as he was raping him. The wee lad managed to give us a reasonable description of the guy and particularly notable was that he had a Teddy boy hairstyle.

We started our investigation but to be honest we weren't getting anywhere. Jimmy and I made enquiries around the toilets but nobody knew anybody of that description, or if they did they certainly weren't telling us. I thought about this wee lad a lot, about the way he had been left, and what had been done to him. Some cases just really get to you. I thought that somebody must know the man we were looking for. I was sure that, for the man we were looking for, it wasn't just a one-off going in there. Sometimes in policework, you just have to use your initiative and get down and dirty. I had to find out what went on in that 'other world'. I decided the only thing I could do was to go undercover.

I went about the city centre for a day or two, and went down into all the public toilets in the town to have a piss. I was just hanging about the sort of place I thought he might turn up, looking to see if I could find anybody who fitted the description we had. I was in one of the toilets this day and I started talking to the boy that looked after them. He was washing out the toilets, mopping the floor. I said, 'There's a big fella used to come in here, I never see him now at all. He must have gone away somewhere. He used to have a Teddy boy haircut and clothes. I just can't remember where the bloody hell he lives.' It's strange the underworld that goes on round you that you know nothing about. The cleaner, obviously thinking I'm a friend of his, turns to me and said, 'It's been a week or two since he's been down here.' I said, 'Where is it he lives anyway?' He said, 'More than likely he's back up in his place in Sandy Row,' then he named this street.

I went back to the station to see Jimmy and told him that we might have a lead on this bastard from the toilets. We went back to the toilet to speak to the cleaner more formally, pushing him a bit harder for more detailed answers. He came up with a name and address. I decided to go and visit the boy the cleaner had named. Your man opened the door and he was the dead ringer for what the wee lad described. He was a Teddy boy and he was wearing a blazer with silver buttons and grey trousers. No doubt this was our man. We brought him in. He wasn't admitting anything, so we decided to put him in an identity parade. The inspector agreed to put him in the parade. When the wee lad went in to see if he could pick him out of the line-up, he jumped in behind the inspector and started to cry. He was terrified. The inspector had to reassure the young lad to get him to go through the formal procedure of the parade. The wee lad pointed straight away to your man and I charged him. He put a bail application in at his court appearance. As usual, of course, bail was granted. I had objected to bail in the strongest possible terms but he got it anyway. He never appeared again. He did a disappearing act.

Years later, I was uniform sergeant in Strandtown Station in east Belfast when I got a call telling me this boy had been arrested in England. It was our friend. I went over and brought him back to Belfast. I went out to see the victim, who was obviously our main witness, to tell him what I thought was good news. We'd charged the guy and all. The wee lad was now a married man. He had children of his own and he had blocked what had happened. He didn't want to go to court. I even tried to do your man for jumping bail but the DPP [director of public prosecutions] just said it's not cost-effective.

A bastard like that buggering a wee kid, ruined him basically for life, and he walks free. It's funny how things like that turn out. That guy should never have got bail, but that was a regular occurrence. The courts were a joke sometimes, more like a pantomime. It's very frustrating as a policeman to have to watch someone like that walk free.

15:04 – CID Office, Woodburn Police Station, West Belfast

IRA bomb scares used to cause havoc in the city centre. You used to have a transit van full of police that went around, continually clearing the streets because you always had a bomb warning. Particularly on Thursdays, for some reason. A bomb scare blocked up the whole city centre. In the mornings you had a bomb scare, and maybe in the afternoons you had another just before rush hour when people were trying to get home. I never saw the point of it from the IRA's perspective. It just pissed people off from both sides of the divide. It was cheap to do, though, and minor risk to the terrorist.

I remember one day leaving Woodburn to head back home. As soon as I got on to the motorway, there were disruptions from bomb scares. Four hours I sat on that fucking motorway going nowhere. I was not a happy person!

One thing you did have to watch for were bomb scares in the same place. The IRA would watch to see where you put the cordons and the ICP [incident control point]. Then you would get a bomb scare with a booby trap for police dealing with it. Several police officers were murdered or injured at just such a road closing from standing at the same place out of habit.

15:06 – Special Branch Office, Belfast

The members of Special Branch were involved constantly in recruiting informers – or agents, as they became once they were established and proven to have access to one of the paramilitary organisations we were targeting. Targeted groups were principally the UVF and the UDA on the loyalist side. On the republican side, the Provisional IRA, the INLA and so on. This was the bread and butter of Special Branch's work. Ideally you got information to stop the incident taking place and save lives. Throughout my period in the Branch, the overwhelming thing was to save life. That was our *raison d'être*.

When the Branch first started out in the early 1970s, the whole idea was simply to be able to tell the government of the day, along with the chief constable, what was going to happen. Later that changed, because the traditional methods of people coming forward as witnesses stopped working. The IRA intimidated witnesses and juries. The intimidation was either direct or indirect. If a witness was determined to testify, the intimidation moved to their families. The net result was people wouldn't give the police statements, and they wouldn't come into court and give evidence. They knew they were going to die if they did.

In some ways this tactic backfired, because it caused the Branch to change to counter the intimidation. The Branch became more pre-emptive. It also started to have surveillance capacity, coupled with having a uniform element who actually arrested people in the act of committing the offence. That said, the overwhelming drive for the force was to recruit agents who could tell you something. The best people to recruit were actually in these target organisations. The motivating factors for the terrorist were many and varied. Money was a big motivating factor. For the majority of them, I'd say it was money. Occasionally it was revenge because they had been slighted by somebody.

Of course, recruitment wasn't the preserve of Special Branch – it happened across the board. A classic example of that was the time the IRA recruited that oul' boy Owen Connolly, who was a retired civil servant that used to work in Stormont. He was an ex-RAF guy, a war hero. He lived at Campbell Park Avenue off the Newtownards Road and he targeted an assistant prison governor. He then told the IRA that the boy lived off the Belmont Road and that every morning he checked under his car before driving to work. He put the IRA gun team up in his house the night before and night after the murder. The IRA team, including a female, came over from north Belfast and killed their victim in his driveway when he was checking under his car for booby traps. They then hid out in Connolly's house until police activity had settled down. Connolly assisted the terrorists in every way he could, even walking with them to the bus stop when they made their escape.

His motivating factor was revenge. He was a Catholic who was employed in the civil service but thought he should have been promoted higher than he was. He perceived that he had been badly treated and that's what drove him to jeopardise his family, including his daughter's future, and involve them all in murder, for which he received a life sentence.

Some who we recruited in the IRA were ideologically driven to join. But the more they saw, they eventually realised it was wrong. They got to the point where they wanted to do something to help stop it. Other factors would include a sense of importance, a sense of excitement; they wanted to be like James Bond or something. Others would just say yes to the last person who spoke to them. These people didn't make good agents. They basically were weak individuals. Certainly as the years went on what amazed me was the sheer number of people in both the loyalist and IRA organisations who at one time or another worked for us. Some people worked for us for twenty or thirty years. They were career informants rather than terrorists.

Some of the informants who were recruited very early on ended up gaining high rank in their organisations. It's often been said to me how it really is incredible every time another big name has been exposed. Two of the so-called big ones frequently mentioned are Stakeknife, and

Denis Donaldson from the Sinn Féin office in Stormont – but actually most of the names that have been exposed wouldn't have been in the top fifty.

People's value went up and down depending on the position they held. We deliberately made sure we didn't know the identity of sources unless we had to know. But I can tell you some of those boys that have been exposed were not important agents, not in the bigger scheme of things. As the Troubles went on, some of the big players were informants because they wanted an end to the trouble. I was talking to a former colleague the other day who debriefed a very senior IRA man several years after the Good Friday Agreement. He said to him, 'Why did you come to the peace table?' He replied, 'It's simple – you were winning the intelligence war. We were so riddled with informants that people weren't prepared to do things, there was no light at the end of the tunnel.'

There were certain areas where the penetration was actually very slight. There were others where it was very, very large. The penetration was never as good as you wanted. You always wanted more. There were times when we wouldn't have put effort into recruiting into a certain area, because the coverage was already so good. Even if one of the agents had been exposed, or had to leave the country, there were two or three ready to replace him.

If there had been enough informants, we would have stopped the killing totally. I think one of the reasons why we managed to negate the loyalist organisations so totally was because the penetration was pretty comprehensive. That's why they killed relatively few people. A lot of lives were saved by agents on both sides.

15:08 – CID Office, North Belfast

I was off duty one day, drinking in the bar in the town I lived in. A lot of the local people in it knew I was a policeman. This man who was a regular came up to me. Billy the Tiler he was known as, because that's what he worked at. He said to me, 'You're in the police, aren't you?' I said, 'Yes,' and then he asked me if I knew this particular detective. I did know him and indeed I worked with him, knew him quite well. But you are always wary when you get asked things like that. You don't know what's coming next. The tiler said, 'He's a desperate big man.' I said, 'Why do you say that?' It transpired that a couple of years before, the tiler had been working in a club in Belfast as a barman. One night some guys came in to rob it when it was closing. They had taken Billy and locked him in the drinks store, which to be honest I thought he would have been happy enough about, while they robbed the place.

They emptied all the drink stock out and all the cash and cigarettes they could find. He told me the detectives must have thought it was an inside job. So poor Billy got brought in. This guy he mentioned interviewed him. Now he was a fairly tough interviewer, I have to say. I've see him interviewing and he was very good at what he did. But the wee tiler, who was as honest as the day was long, was baffled by the whole experience. He just kept saying, 'Desperate man, desperate man.' I said, 'What was the problem?' He said, 'He went on at me and he had me convinced, I was absolutely convinced, that I'd been involved in the robbery. The only thing that stopped me making a statement about it was I couldn't work out how I did it.' I suppose it's a good example of the powers of persuasion.

15:22 – Cookstown Police Station, County Tyrone

A policeman I was stationed with came from a nationalist area. He was a Catholic officer and his family still lived in the area he was originally from. It was always very difficult for policemen from that background to return home. Simple things like going to see their parents and family. They would be particularly targeted by republican terror groups as a deterrent to others thinking of joining. They were giving up a lot by joining and I always admired their courage. In many cases, members of their family would disown them and never speak to them again. This officer's father had sadly died and neither him nor his brother, who was a prison officer, were able to attend their own father's funeral. It was too dangerous. I remember that day well, going into a bar and meeting him and his brother. I didn't know his dad had passed away. I got a pint and was just chatting to them. I said, 'Well, how's things going?' He said, 'My father's being buried.' All he could do was sit and drink. He couldn't even go to say goodbye to his dad. Those were the very sad and tragic things about the job. It happened to many people, but when you know the people personally it's hard. My heart went out to them both.

15:23 – At the Dogs

We had gone to a greyhound racing track away up in the middle of nowhere. The guy I was working with knew Billy, the owner, and he had heard that Billy had come into a fair chunk of money that day. The idea was that he was going to have a few celebratory drinks with him. We went in, spoke to Billy, and he asked us if we'd like a drink.

I had a good look around. There were about thirty-odd men playing snooker, plus quite a few standing at the bar having a drink. I also noticed that everybody in the place was male, no females about at all. I didn't drink that day – I was on soft drinks. We had been in about twenty minutes. My friend was chatting to the man that owned it, who was serving behind the counter. The next thing my friend was approached by a man with a squashed nose, harelip, ugly-looking guy. But a big fella. He looked into my friend's face and he said, 'Do you remember me?' My friend looked him straight in the eye and said, 'Why? Should I?' Yer man said, 'Oh aye, you called me a Provo bastard in a cell one time.' He just looked at him and said, 'Wasn't I right?' I nearly fell off the chair because I was thinking, we are vastly outnumbered here.

Little did I know just how dangerous a situation we were in. Your man then sloped off back to his mates. I could see he was obviously telling them what had been said. If they hadn't known already who we were, he was obviously making it clear we were police. I saw him go down towards a public phone near the door. The next thing another drink was set up, and I was set up with a vodka and Coke. I looked at it and thought, 'He doesn't think I'm drinking, does he?' Sure I was on soft drinks. I said to the man I was with, my sergeant, 'Billy's after giving me a drink.' My colleague then said, 'Right, out! Let's go.' I said, 'What?' He said, 'Get the car!' So I said okay. My friend – he had changed colour. He was very worried-looking. He repeated, 'Get the car,' which was a wee unmarked police vehicle parked over on the corner.

I got the motor, and picked him up at the front door. We headed off down the road but met a car coming in, a big motor with the lights on inside. We passed them as they were turning in, and I noticed a lot of heads in it. I turned left at the end of the lane and away we went. I didn't know things had got pretty serious until the next day. The sergeant I had been with came to me and said, 'I don't want to be worrying you, but I got a pull from the authorities over our visit up to the dog track.' I said, 'What do you mean?' He asked me, 'Do you remember that car that turned into the lane when we were leaving?' I said, 'Aye, I do. The one with the lights and all on.' He

said, 'That was a car-load of IRA men.' After we had just
left they came into the bar, took over the entire place and
were looking for us. He said, 'Don't be worrying yourself,
because I haven't said anybody was with me.' I said, 'You're
joking.' He was worried the bosses would have been angry
at him for being there, taking a drink. He wasn't as worried
that armed men had come in to kill us! He didn't drop me
in it. He told them he was there on business, because it was
all part and parcel of making contact with the criminal
elements. You had to be seen amongst them. Thank God
the owner was on the ball. He couldn't risk telling us what
he'd overheard on the phone call, so he gave us both the
wrong drinks hoping that we'd catch on. Fortunately my
sergeant did. A fortnight later we were back in the place.

15:24 – Special Branch Headquarters, Belfast

This concerns a phone call I received from a senior officer
in the Garda. He was phoning from Dublin. It was around
the early summer of 2000. He told me there had been a
shooting incident in Dublin about April or May. A guy had
been shot dead by the PIRA [Provisional IRA]. The Guards
now knew that it was the Provisionals. The dead man's name
was Thomas Byrne. The Provisionals were on a ceasefire
at the time, and the political talks in relation to Northern
Ireland were at a very tense stage. Bertie Ahern was taoiseach
and was very involved in the ongoing negotiations.

The Irish government were doing everything they could
to protect the PIRA and to push their agenda through, i.e.
there had to be talks without decommissioning of arms.
That was one of the major stumbling blocks at the time.
The unionists were insisting on decommissioning and
the republicans were against it. The parties were talking,
attempting to reach a compromise.

This Garda officer explained that what had happened

was the boy who had been murdered had been in a fight before Christmas the previous year with a leading member of the IRA in Dublin. Byrne had given this IRA man a good hammering, and as a result, the PIRA had ordered him to be exiled out of the country. Not an uncommon occurrence in the north. The guy had fled to Spain and after a while his mother had made some approaches to Sinn Féin to see if he could come back. She offered to pay a sort of fine to let him back in. But they wouldn't have it, because they were trying to make everybody scared of them.

Byrne did come back around February when he lived quite openly in Dublin for about two months. I think eventually money did change hands, which made him think he would be safe. One night, they'd put chairs and tables outside this pub in north Dublin he drank in. It was a normal Friday evening at O'Neill's pub in the Summerhill area and the bar was pretty busy. Byrne was having a beer with some friends outside and somebody just walked past on foot, bang and he was shot in the head. He died at the scene. The lone gunman walked around the corner, jumped into a car and was away. It was all over in a matter of seconds. The car – all this was explained to me by this officer in the guards – was found burnt out about a couple of miles away. The problem for the IRA was that the car had not totally ignited. Only half of it had burnt out and the bit that hadn't burnt out contained the petrol container which had been used to spread the petrol around the car before they lit the match. Everybody knew from the word go that it was the PIRA.

One of the Garda investigating officers thought, 'Who would you use to kill a boy in broad daylight in the centre of Dublin?' Logically, he thought you wouldn't use a Dublin IRA man. Everyone would know them, and the people at the pub might recognise a local. It would make more sense to use a clean skin from Northern Ireland. An experienced killer, who would be brought over the border, do the business and back across the border. The trail would be cold in no time. They despatched a couple of Garda up towards the border. This was before the motorway. They told them to check every filling station between there and the border to see if any of them had CCTV, which might show either the car or somebody filling a container with petrol. There only were three or four petrol stations in the area. And there it was on the CCTV. Pictures of at least one of the individuals involved in the murder. The whole car they had used could be seen and him filling the very same container which was used to set fire to the getaway vehicle after the shooting. My first question was, 'What's the quality of the CCTV film like?' Because usually in those days it was an old VHS tape machine which had been used three hundred times and was wiped every twenty-four hours. People would spend thousands on these systems but not replace the tapes for the sake of a pound, making them useless. He said, 'You could count the hairs in his eyebrows. His full face, absolutely no question about it. It's as plain as day, full recognition.' He wanted to know how they could identify this individual. I told them there were two ways. 'One way is you simply send me the photograph, I'll have it copied, put on a poster, sent out within twenty-four hours to be seen by every police officer we have. Within another twenty-four hours, you'll have your suspect identified because it really will go to every police station.' We had 150 police establishments in the RUC and it would go to them all. It would just take one person who knows him to look at the poster in the station and say, 'Oh yes, that's Joe Bloggs.' But it is noisy – everyone will know we are looking for this boy. I said, 'If you want it done really quietly, you give the footage to me, I copy it, not so many copies. But I will send them to all the Special Branch offices and the agent handlers will know him. He is obviously an active terrorist so the Branch in his area should know him.'

If the handlers didn't know him, and they tended to know every terrorist in their area, one of their agents would. It would take a few days or even a week. If it was a totally clean skin, somebody we had never come across, it could take longer, but somebody out there would know.

The Garda officer kept saying, 'It's political, it's political.' The Garda are much more politically controlled than the RUC were. In the end, he decided he would go away and consult with his bosses and then he would come back and let me know what they were going to do. Nothing ever happened. They never investigated that murder because the IRA were on ceasefire. It wasn't that a follow-up on that video evidence alone was enough to charge someone with murder. But it certainly would have given plenty to talk about. Let us not forget the murder was carried out in broad daylight and in front of a number of witnesses.

How would you feel if you were a close relative or family member of Thomas Byrne? It certainly wasn't dropped because the individual Garda wanted to pull the plug. It was the political pressure pure and simple. No one to this day has been charged with the murder. I think it was disgusting and in all my time in the RUC I never heard of anything like that; political pressure controlling the police.

15:25 – Carrickmore Police Station, County Tyrone

There was a guy in Carrickmore, an awful nice man, a single man. He'd been a teacher but he joined the police. He wanted to find his fame and glory, so he applied for Carrickmore. He didn't realise exactly what it was all about down there. He rang up to ask how to get to the station and I explained it was too dangerous to drive and told him he had to get a helicopter from Omagh. 'You go to St Lucia Camp, park your car up and the boys will keep you right. Bring your changes of clothes with you because you will be in here for four days at a time.' That's the way the shifts worked – you were on for four days, off for two.

When he arrived, instead of having something like the rest of the boys, a kit bag or a rucksack, this guy had a suitcase. He bails into the helicopter and of course didn't know where he was going. He probably thought he was going to Vietnam or something. Maybe he had been watching too many war movies. In a Lynx helicopter, you had the loadmaster, who checked for electricity pylons that could be obstructions, and to see if it's safe to take off and land. He communicated with the pilot, especially in relation to the rotor, because the pilot obviously can't see behind. So off they went from Omagh to the station, nine boys in the helicopter. As they were coming in to land, standard procedure was the loadmaster opened the door and then he would have had a look out to make sure the landing was clear before touching down. They were hovering at about twenty feet. The ex-teacher, exactly as he might have seen it in the movies, he immediately bailed out with his suitcase. The suitcase opened, and underpants and socks, everything was blown all over the place in the downdraft. He broke both his ankles and wasn't seen for three months. That was his baptism into life in Carrickmore.

15:27 – Uniform Patrol, West Belfast

We were sitting in the canteen at Woodburn when we got a call down to Andersonstown Police Station. A suspect device had just been abandoned outside the front. I had the inspector with me. We were the first to arrive. We immediately started clearing the houses, making sure there was nobody in danger. You rapped the door, looking in through the windows to see if there was any movement. I was moving down the street repeating that at every house. The inspector was practically down at the corner and that's when that thing went off. It was a massive explosion, the bomb weighed 1,000lb.

The force of the blast put me on my back. This massive cloud of dust and glass came up the road. Lucky enough I was at a door and not a window. If I had been at a window, my good looks might have been ruined. But I went down with a terrible pain in my leg. This was one of my worst fears, because anytime a bomb went off, you always did a check for the arms and fingers, and down the legs, to make sure everything was still there. I didn't want to put my hand down because I could feel the pain. I couldn't bring myself to look down. Then all of a sudden the second crew arrived. I got up, not a mark on me. I think it was a bit of rubber from a tyre that had hit me. There wasn't a wound or anything.

There were other police in the sanger in Andytown Station. Special Branch surveillance were waiting in the sanger, watching for the bomb to arrive. But fucked off before it exploded. They knew exactly what was going on, but they never bothered to tell us. It was no thanks to them that we weren't killed. The station sergeant didn't leave his post. He came out after the blast, his hair grey, because the ceilings came down.

Big Alan lost his eye, and his turtle-shell body armour looked like a hedgehog it had been hit so many times with shrapnel. He was lucky he wasn't killed. I can actually remember on the news, one of the headlines was Sinn Féin condemned the closing of the road and stopping people getting to and from work.

I recall another murder when I was stationed in Antrim Road. It was up at the top of the Crumlin Road, as you head out of the city into the country. It took place in a small video rental shop. The victim was a young Protestant boy working there. He was sixteen years of age. I was in the CID office that night, when the call came in that there had been a shooting. Unfortunately an all-too-common occurrence up there. I made my way up to the scene to see what the score was. It was a long night. He was murdered by the INLA, no great reason. Just in the wrong place at the wrong time, like many others.

I made sure all the relevant agencies had been tasked, scenes of crime people, photography branch and the like. It was just like everything else you attend. You try, probably subconsciously, to distance yourself from the horrible things you see at the crime scene, and just get on with it. It's a sort of self-defence mechanism to remain that wee bit detached or you'd go mad.

The detective inspector called up to the scene. He said he wanted me to go over and see the parents of the victim the next day. When I got there, the body had been returned, having been embalmed after the post-mortem had been carried out. They lived in a Housing Executive house. I noticed how beautifully kept it was, absolutely immaculate. Unfortunately, there was only one downstairs room, an open-plan living room and kitchen. The corpse was lying in the coffin in the living room. Only then did it hit home to me that this was a son, this young boy was a really loved son. It affected me so much that I couldn't take the statement. It was weird the way it suddenly really got to me. Also the woman was of very strong Christian faith, and she said to me, 'I'll pray for these people that murdered my son.' I just couldn't cope with that. I had to arrange to go back and see his mum after he was buried. It was just so bloody tragic. It still brings a tear to my eye even now all these years later.

16:32 – Uniform Patrol, Randalstown Road, County Antrim

It's not just terrorist things that can be very tragic and upsetting. I remember going to a triple fatal accident on the Randalstown Road in Antrim. Three young men all in the one car. It was a horrific accident. They hit a wall. Why, I don't know. I was the supervising sergeant. The driver and the front-seat passenger were obviously dead but the impact was of such magnitude that the fire brigade was called to cut them out. The young fellow in the back, you could hear muffled groans coming from him. He was still alive but you couldn't get at him. The fire brigade did their best, but by the time they got him out he was dead. That horrific scene lasted for about twenty minutes. I knew what the outcome was going to be and I could do nothing about it, other than stand there and watch him die. At the post-mortem the next day, the cause of death was asphyxiation. If he had been released earlier, he would have lived. But the front passenger seat was pushed so far back on to him. That is still something I see in my sleep to this day.

16:33 – Uniform Patrol, County Londonderry

This happened during the hunger strike in 1981. It's quite a funny wee story. During that time, tensions were running high throughout the country. The place was a tinderbox. The slightest thing could spark widespread rioting. As usual, the police were stuck in the middle. Tricolours were placed in practically every nationalist town and village. One wee nationalist village in County Derry, there was nearly a tricolour hanging from every post. The street with all the flags on it was a main thoroughfare for both sides – nationalist and unionist.

The next village along was a very staunch unionist village and people had been on the phone to the sub-divisional commander complaining about the flags. They threatened that if nothing was done about it, the locals would go up and remove them. This would have made the situation ten times worse. Faced with this dilemma, the sub-divisional commander rang the local sergeant and said, 'I want all tricolours down in your area. All of them. I don't care how you get them down, but get them down from that main road.' A couple of constables went out, and they just pulled them down. But there was one we were particularly worried about because the tricolour wasn't on a wooden pole it was actually on a metal pole. We were concerned the pole was maybe booby-trapped. One of the constables had an automatic shotgun, so we said, 'Go back and get your shotgun and we'll shoot this flag to blazes.' The constable went back to the station to get the gun. The constable, by the way, had just been the day before to stores [police uniform stores] in Belfast to get a new uniform and a new cap. When we got back to the flag post, he fired a couple of shots at the tricolour to try and blast it off. He went to fire the third shot, and just as he did, the sergeant took his cap off him and threw it up into the air. It was blown to bits. The rest of us were in tears. His face was a picture.

16:36 – Border Checkpoint, Dublin Road, Newry

Newry had a permanent vehicle checkpoint in place, on the Dublin Road near the border. The army would fly the police and troops to man it in and out. They were never in cars, it would have been too dangerous. It was the main Belfast to Dublin route and a very busy road. The checkpoint operated twenty-four hours and like everywhere else in Northern Ireland, but particularly because it was static, it had its dangers. Every now and then, Special Branch would receive intelligence warning of various levels of threat. One day we got information in and were told to come off the road as an attack was imminent. We were happy enough, because we were able to go up into the wee cube, and it's well armoured, a place of safety.

They didn't say the imminent attack was going to be on us. I thought it was going to be somewhere in the south Armagh area. But it was specifically us. They fired a mortar at the checkpoint. All the alarms went off after the explosion. We were sitting playing Monopoly when it happened. There were three or four of us and then the army, who were always with us at the checkpoint. They had their own bits and pieces of kit all round the room. As you sat down, you'd have set stuff around the room. Your flak jacket down here, gun belt there and your hat someplace else. See when that mortar bomb went off? You literally felt the blast coming up through the ground. We didn't know if it was the start of a sustained attack or a one-off. The three or four of us were running about like headless chickens in this wee room looking for our kit. I thought, 'Forget about it. They'll not find anything of their stuff in the mess and confusion.'

I went up into the front office room to see if I could find out what was happening. This army lieutenant, young guy, probably his first tour of duty here, said, 'Right, get the QRF [quick reaction force] out, do your outer cordon.' I said, 'Hang on, just hang on a minute. Wait until we have eyes in the sky. Wait until the choppers arrive from Bessbrook. They are only a few minutes away.' I added, 'Inner cordon, yes, not outside. Do not go outside, because we don't know what's there. We're safe here for now.' They found the crater where one of mortars had exploded when it came down on one of the security cameras around the post. It had landed on the road a hundred yards short of the checkpoint. The lieutenant was going, 'I have to get out to the thing.' I said, 'Don't.' Then the army sergeant said, 'I have to agree with the policeman. It would be stupid sending somebody out.'

In the end he didn't send anybody out, just as well too. We waited until the choppers were in the air and they found traces of somebody waiting with a heavy machine gun right down the road. We probably saved a couple of soldiers' lives that day. They were waiting there for us to come running out after the attack. It could have been the .50 man [sniper], because he was running about there at that time. Either way, someone would have died if we had gone out.

17:11 – Uniform Patrol, North Belfast

We got a call to a shooting over in the Oldpark area of Belfast. When we arrived, there wasn't much sign of anything, which was common enough. A few people milling around, but that was it. Nothing seemed out of the ordinary. You were always very cautious about these sort of calls in case it's a come-on. I headed over to the actual address to see what was going on. But there was no sign of any 'victim'. I made my way slowly into the house, gun drawn, listening and looking for anything out of the ordinary. I saw this pool of blood at the bottom of the stairs. Then I saw more blood on the steps and I started to follow the trail upstairs. As I turned on to the landing, there was a man sitting on a chair with his hands pressed against his stomach. Blood was oozing out between his fingers. He'd been shot. I walked towards him and he looked up at me and just said, 'Fuck, that was close!' Turned out two guys had called at the house and tried to kill him. But the gun jammed after they got the first shot off!

17:19 – Carrickmore Police Station, County Tyrone

On 21 December 1985 there was a big threat on in Carrickmore, which was more or less the norm to tell you the truth. Two routes had been cleared in and out. Two hundred combined army and police personnel were searching the whole of the Carrickmore area, so patrols and manpower could get in and out.

Every morning, the police cleared two routes out of Carrickmore, so that there was an alternative route if they were being observed by terrorists at one. There were only three routes in. One from the Creggan, one from Ballintree and one from Sixmilecross. We had information there was going to be a mortar attack on the station. The whole place had been swamped with police from about 5.30 a.m. All the Carrickmore triangle was searched. They were out at it all day, and as a result there was only a skeleton crew left in the station.

Normally there would have been two patrol sections in at any given time, plus the neighbourhood beat guys. But because of the threat there was only myself and eight guys. There was plenty of accommodation at the station, but it was all Portakabins. There were no mortar-proof bunkers in those days. The communications office was an old rectory.

They'd searched all day and nothing had been found. At about 5.00 p.m., just as it was getting dark, the whole convoy headed off back to Omagh. Half an hour later, I was in one of the Portakabins and I thought, 'I'll just nip out to the toilet.' I got into the toilet and I heard this loud noise. Some of the guys had accidental discharges with their weapons now and again, you know, messing about.

I thought, some of those boys have been messing about again and they've let off a round. Then there was like a bit of a thump and this blinding flash. I'm sitting using the loo, and all the air is taken out of the room and I'm blown forward. This mark-10 mortar had landed about five or six yards away and had gone off. The lights went out. I got up, piss and shit all over the place. I literally thought it was my last movement, but luckily I wasn't badly hurt. I then went back into the communications room to call in the attack, then it went quiet. You couldn't really do much in case there were snipers.

Then at first light in the morning you could start piecing together what happened. Six mortars had been launched from the community centre, which was 180 yards away from the station. Luckily, the third mortar stuck in the launch tube and when it exploded it took the rest of the mortars with it. So there was only actually two that landed in the station. Thirty years in the police, and my main recurring memory is a visit to the loo. We were just very lucky nobody was killed or seriously injured.

17:32 – Uniform Patrol, West Belfast

We were driving along the Stewartstown Road. We were told there was a suspect device. It was a trailer bomb just up the road that we had driven by. They had detonated it, but it didn't go off. One of the guys who was fairly new to the crew said he thought he had seen some suspicious activity. But he didn't want to say anything in case we laughed at him.

We found out later, after the forensics had been done, that the bomb had been set and triggered, but it didn't go off. It probably would have taken out the whole three crews, every one of us. When they were disarming it, the controlled explosion set part of it off and the blast put the hitch of the trailer through the roof of a house about 200 yards away. I dread to think of the carnage if it had gone off as intended, as we were driving past it.

18:11 – CID Office, Belfast City Centre

A few of us from Antrim Road CID were at work one night and decided we'd go down to Botanic Avenue for an Indian. We were sitting up the stairs in this restaurant and we were just about to get tucked into our starter. I spotted a uniformed sergeant talking to the waiter over by the door. I thought it a bit strange and wondered what's this about? I went across and said to him, 'Is there an issue?' He said, 'There's a threat on to come here and shoot you three. They've spotted you coming in here and they're coming down now to shoot you.' I said, 'Can we not get our starter?' He said, 'No, I think you'd better go now.'

We said they can't be coming that quick. But eventually he convinced us. So we walked downstairs and out, and they had the whole street sealed off. I suppose we shouldn't have been there having our tea. Me and Bogie Boyd went straight back to Antrim Road and said we didn't want this in the duty officer's report. So he managed somehow to remove any incident happening in the area and we got away with it.

I think back and can't believe what was going on in our heads. Is that how used we had become to things? We were arguing about leaving instead of being grateful that they got the information that undoubtedly saved our lives. The murder team was actually on its way and we were refusing to leave, arguing over eating a curry.

18:15 – Crossmaglen Police Station, County Armagh

I moved out to Crossmaglen Station for the rebuilding of it after it had been bombed. It's in south Armagh, very close to the border with the Republic of Ireland. Bandit country.

They would regularly move people around after an attack on a station to help secure the area and allow workmen to repair damage. I wasn't there very long when they opened fire at us, fired at our permanent checkpoint in the town.

We got a report of an imminent attack from Special Branch so they pushed our quick reaction force one hundred yards down the road away from the permanent vehicle checkpoint to get a better view of the danger zone. One of the guys notices a car acting a bit oddly just down the street. This is when the Provos were in the habit of firing at us from the boot of a car with the sniper lying in it.

The QRF was about five or six men but they would have had a rocket grenade launcher with them. They were dug in and camouflaged so they were able to watch this car and not be seen. When it turned at the bottom of the street, the brake lights came on. QRF are looking along their gun sights at this car, only to see a guy looking through a gun sight back at them. The brake lights had lit up the inside of the boot. They could see him as clear as day.

The sniper had just opened the boot up slightly and was looking through the sight towards them. They started shooting at him. The policeman who reacted first must have had tracer rounds at the top of his magazine. I don't know if they would ignite the rocket or whether it needed a live round to ignite it, but he was going like mad trying to get a round off because it was all tracers at the start.

One of the other men was whacking away at the car. He hit the car, because part of it came off. But they had it armour-plated around the sniper. But if our guy had managed to get that rocket off, if it had landed anywhere near the car, they would have had them. We were so close and would have saved many lives, but luck was with the terrorist. The Provo just panicked and opened fire anyway. He hit the Sinn Féin office. I had a bit of a laugh at that.

Bernard Henry McGinn – the sniper concerned – shot dead seven soldiers and two police officers. His reign of terror ended when he was arrested with others at a farmhouse by the SAS. The weapon was recovered with the bulletproof car. He named all the terrorists and operations he was involved with. The explosives expert was sentenced to 490 years in prison for 34 offences. The gang was released under the Good Friday Agreement. He was found dead at a house in Monaghan a short time later.

18:18 – Uniform Patrol, Belfast

We got a call one night to an incident in a housing estate. When we arrived there was one guy lying with a gunshot wound at the front door, and another, a milkman, with a money satchel round his neck. The milkman had arrived at the house to collect the outstanding milk money, as he did every Friday at teatime. He had just rung the bell when a man in a mask arrived with a gun to rob him. The milkman was a part-time member of the Ulster Defence Regiment and automatically assumed the robber was an IRA hitman who was going to try to kill him so he drew his personal protection weapon. Just as this was happening, the householder, having lifted the money from the mantelpiece, opened the front door to pay his bill. This startled the milkman, who immediately opened fire. He missed the gunman, but seriously wounded his customer in the chest while the gunman escaped.

A few days later, I called at the hospital to see the man who had been shot and find out how he was getting on. We were sitting chatting about what happened and he said, 'There was no need for that. I was only a week behind.' At least he hadn't lost his Belfast sense of humour, although he nearly lost his life.

19:37 – CID Office, Antrim Road Police Station, North Belfast

My colleague Victor, he was a detective, and rather than sit in the office all the time and do paperwork, we would always go out in the CID vehicle for a drive round our patch when we got a chance. The car was not armoured, indeed it had no protection whatsoever. It probably stuck out like a sore thumb, plus we wore shirts and ties. I suppose we weren't very covert or sensible, but we always went out for a patrol round, looking for stolen vehicles or anything out of the ordinary. It was good for our local knowledge.

One night, we heard a call to a uniform patrol to go immediately to Joanmount Park. There were reports that a man had been shot. As we weren't that far away, we went. We actually got there before the ambulance and police tasked to go officially. We were first on the scene. We went into the house to find Jim Peacock, a prison officer, had been shot dead. He was lying on the kitchen floor with his wife in hysterics, along with his daughter. We were trying as CID officers to clear the area where the shooting had taken place for preservation of the scene.

We were also trying to calm the woman down, while trying to elicit stuff from her to establish what exactly she had seen. That's one of the few times as a detective I was first there. Mostly when CID arrive at the scene, police are already there and the initial panic is gone and the area is all sealed off, secure. Your role at that stage is to sort of organise and begin the hunt for evidence. This was one occasion we knew the scene was definitely not contaminated.

That was quite harrowing to try and deal with that poor woman. I mean, she was standing there, watching her husband die in front of her. We were there to try and help her through that and you're not trained in those skills. That just comes with experience and you try your best. Things like that stick with you for a long, long time. It turned out it was actually loyalists who shot him. They were having a problem with the prison officers.

20:32 – Special Branch Office, Belfast

One informant I had from west Belfast worked for me for a very long time, and he used to gather incredible information about terrorist crime, and indeed some ordinary crime. But terrorist crime was where his strength lay. He was working on a specific task for me, gathering information in relation to the murder of a policeman in west Belfast. I happened to be in another police station across the city and heard some cops talking about a raid that was due to take place in a house in south Belfast that night. It was being organised by the drug squad. I knew it was quite likely 'my man' would be at that party. So I spoke to one of the bosses involved in the operation to see if I could go along. I had to get myself involved in the raid because there was every possibility that he would be arrested and I needed him back on the street. Of course I couldn't tell all the police involved why.

What he was doing at the time was very important and, to be honest, whether he was smoking a joint or not at a party didn't really come into it. It was a judgement call but he was getting information for me in relation to a murder and obviously that takes precedence over anything that may have occurred at the party. It was a fairly big raid. There were a lot of police personnel involved. The target premises was a three-storey terraced house. The flat we were interested in was on the top floor.

The army were also involved, supplying night sun – which is the big spotlight to light an area up, allowing police to prevent escape from the premises – from a helicopter. They had two prison vans organised to take the people that would be arrested to the police office for processing.

When the raid started I went up and entered the top floor with other police in plain clothes. Sure enough, my man was sitting there. I went over and arrested him, actually quite aggressively because it had to look good for his mates. I slapped what he was smoking out of his mouth, and grabbed him by the shoulder to pull him up. I was sort of trailing him out of the flat to get him out and over to the top of the stairs. Of course no one else taking part in the raid knew what I was doing. I'm sure a few wondered why I was there in the first place. I got him to the top of the stairs to discover that the divisional mobile support unit, or riot police, had lined the stairs the entire way up all three floors. When I came out with my man, they obviously thought that he had been fighting with me and resisting arrest. Unfortunately, they took over to pass him on down one to the other. They kicked the shit clean out of him the whole way down the stairs, while I'm trying to shout and whisper at the same time, 'No, no, no!'

When he got to the bottom he was lying there in a mangled heap on the ground. He had been kneecapped before by the IRA, and his leg was all over the place, sticking out at right angles from the knee down. I got him up and I must say he took it all very well. He actually thought the rougher it was, the better it looked for him in front of the others. As I was taking him out to the prison van I said, 'You just keep your mouth shut,' which he did. I went to the police office where he was taken to be processed, got him booked in, and then once everything had settled down, and all his mates were tucked up in their cells, I went back over and got him released. I drove him back to west Belfast to get him back on to the street.

He got the names of the IRA men involved (it was actually a mortar attack), as well as all the other information I needed, detailed to the point that he was able to tell me where they had taken the sand from to put in bags at the base of the mortar to stabilise it. It was stolen from a children's play park in Belfast. Three persons were taking the sand and filling the bags when an army patrol had actually walked past through the park. They had to abandon the playground area and hide until the patrol left. It's little nuggets of information like that which are very detailed that become particularly useful once you've got the terrorists arrested for questioning. It worries them and obviously implies that you knew more than you are letting on. He was a very good informant. That's just another day in the life of an informant. It's a dangerous game. If they suspect anything you're dead.

20:52 – CID Office, Strand Road Police Station, Londonderry

I have a friend who is an ex-Garda. He is a very humorous sort of character. I remember him relating a story to me of when he was a young Garda in Dublin and he had a case up in court. I can't remember what it was exactly – perhaps an assault. But anyway it was contested and he lost the case.

Later that day he was in the pub having a few pints, and he fell in with this very experienced detective sergeant out of the same Garda station, who had also been at the court on another case that day. The sergeant said to him, 'Joe, I saw you at court today and you didn't have much success in that case you had up. I'll tell you what: you went about it the wrong way. The way you go about this type of thing is you don't start from when the offence commenced. You start at the court case. Then you have to think, now, I want this man convicted of an assault. How do I get this conviction? So you work your way backwards slowly, slowly, slowly to see what evidence you need at the start. You work your way back.'

Joe, quite shocked at what he's hearing, said to him, 'Well, tell me this, sergeant, what about stating what actually happened at the scene, the truth?' The sergeant looked at him for a moment and declared, 'Well, you just attach that to it loosely somewhere along the line.'

20:54 – Woodburn Police Station, West Belfast

In Woodburn, years ago, one of the detectives was going to a fancy dress party, or had been at one. He still had the costume in the station anyway. Things were unusually quiet that day, so they thought they'd play a prank on the detective chief inspector. There's nothing more dangerous than bored cops. One of the guys goes up to the chief's office and said, 'Boss, you're never going to believe this. We've a nun in, she's been caught shoplifting. The detective sergeant is interviewing her now.' Obviously this wasn't a very common occurrence, so the chief decided to go down to find out what was going on.

In Woodburn Station you could see into the interview room. But when the chief looked, all he could see was the detective sergeant with his back sort of bent forward over the table, talking to the nun. He was shouting at her and generally being pretty aggressive. The nun had her head down and all of a sudden, all you could hear was swearing flying out of the sergeant: 'You dirty, thieving bitch,' and all sorts of stuff like that, and really loud. Then he takes a big swipe and slapped her straight in the face.

The chief nearly passed out, he went pure white. 'Oh my God, you can't do that, you can't do that.' He goes running into the interview room, and stutters, 'Are you all right, love?' All he could think of was the mountain of complaints he could see coming his way.

The chief looks at the nun, who still has her head down and is whimpering, and asks again if she is okay. The nun, or rather John, who has a big moustache, looks up and said,

'Don't call me love.' It was brilliant – you should have seen the chief's face. It was one of the best ones I've seen. He called us everything under the sun.

20:55 – Special Branch Office, Belfast
I was aware that during elections in Northern Ireland, personation [assuming the identity of another person with intent to deceive] was going on. It was organised by republicans. I could only describe it as being done on an industrial scale. It wasn't a case of stealing a few votes here or there. It was systematically going through the electoral register, and looting it every which way from Sunday. They became masters at it.

I was getting all this intelligence coming across my desk from sources in the republican movement across the Province. They would look at the electoral list in republican areas and would then apply for a lot of proxy and postal votes. Then when the envelopes containing the voting papers came out in the post, on their way to the applicant's home, the postman, whether of his own inclination because he was a sympathiser, or through sheer intimidation, would hand over the envelopes to the republicans. They would fill out these proxy and postal votes for their candidate, which meant they had thousands of votes in the tank before the election even took place.

They would also look down the electoral list and see who voted last time and who didn't. They would make up medical cards in the names of the people who hadn't voted. In those days, a Northern Ireland medical card was all you needed to prove identity at elections. They had a printing press that turned out medical cards en masse.

The thing was that when they went into a polling station in, say, a housing estate in Lurgan, Coalisland or west Belfast somewhere, maybe the SDLP guy who was there knew rightly that this is not Mr Sean Bloggs who has just come in. But they are totally intimidated by republicans in the area. They cannot dare point this out to the returning officer in the polling station, because they've got to live in the community. Police officers in the polling stations aren't legally allowed to challenge anyone and had to stand and watch this blatant fraud take place. Very often, the SDLP didn't bother sending people to polling booths, because they knew their car was going to be wrecked, or their handbag would be stolen when they were coming out. Or worse.

Another thing they would do is simply look down the electoral list in the evening and see who hadn't voted by 9 p.m., for example [polls closed at 10 p.m.]. Then they would go out to their homes and would threaten them to go out to vote. In small constituencies, like in council elections, fifty votes could swing a seat. But these people were stealing hundreds and hundreds of votes in each seat. That was one of the reasons why Sinn Féin went from around a rock-solid 12 per cent of those who voted up to about 20 per cent in a very short space of time. It wasn't simply the power of the Sinn Féin leaders' political argument. It was this wholesale personation.

I spoke to a lot of policemen and checked the facts as seen on the ground – to compare this with the information we were receiving in Special Branch. The police of course were present in every polling station in the country. Even when they saw people coming in a fifth time to vote, they were powerless to stop them. It was a ludicrous situation.

I went to our fingerprint people and I asked them, 'Surely nowadays there's some sort of system we could use to identify that a person had voted and stop them coming back to vote again?' They said, 'No, there's no such technology at the moment that could do it.' About a year or so later, I got a call out of the blue and it was one of the fingerprint team. He said, 'We think we've got what you're after. Come on down so you can take a look.' They had all the literature about a machine that could do exactly what we wanted. We looked it up online; it was the early days of looking things up on the internet. They showed me this piece of kit. It would have wiped up the direct vote theft – though not the postal and proxy vote theft. I then wrote a report about it. I sent it up to my boss, who sent it up to the Northern Ireland Office to inform them of this breakthrough. The NIO replied and said, 'Yes, fantastic, thanks very much. We'll send this on to the chief electoral officer for his information.'

About eight months later, my boss met the chief electoral officer at an unrelated meeting and said, 'I'm surprised I didn't hear back from you about that report I sent you through the NIO.' The electoral officer said, 'What are you talking about?' My boss explained the story and what the report was about. The electoral officer said, 'They never sent it to me.' And he said, 'The last thing they want to do at the moment is to cripple Sinn Féin. If we introduced that even in a pilot area, the Sinn Féin vote would crash.'

The authorities were aware of the problem, a cure was pointed out to them and the NIO knocked it on the head to keep Sinn Féin on board. The NIO had decided that Sinn Féin could bring the PIRA with them. And who is to say in the scheme of things that they're not right. But in their headlong rush to embrace Sinn Féin, they destroyed the SDLP and the principles of democracy with them.

20:56 – CID Office, Oldpark and Tennent Street Police Stations, North Belfast

I was a detective in Belfast during the 1970s. I worked in CID in north Belfast. We dealt with every crime except murder. Things were so bad in the area that there was actually a murder squad to deal specifically with that offence. I got a call one night to where a body had been found. But it turned out the person was alive, although he had been very badly beaten. It was a man called Gerard McLaverty. He had been walking down the Cliftonville Road when he got picked up by four men in a taxi, which he noted as sitting ahead of him because the car was pointing the wrong direction.

Two men approached him who claimed to be police officers and pretended they were arresting him, which he believed; he actually went with them. It was nearly midnight. He argued with them, saying he had done nothing to be arrested. But they said they had to take him anyway. They drove him around for a while, eventually heading over towards the Shankill Road. He was taken into a building, a disused doctor's surgery. He was interrogated and tortured there for quite some time by the men.

Strangely when they brought McLaverty into the disused doctor's they still kept up the pretence of being police officers. Although it was very apparent they weren't. As he said himself in his statement, 'We went to the room, the fat man came in behind me and said, "You're staying here." ' They then went on to tell him that they would be back in the morning. But they didn't go anywhere. The driver and the fat man went behind the counter, both came back with sticks, one of which had a nail through it. They started to beat him round the head. He needed to protect himself because he was afraid of it going in his eyes. He was told to get his hands down, and they continued to beat and verbally abuse him until he was squealing with pain. Bizarrely during this torture, and I quote from his statement, 'There was a kettle and a teapot in the room. The driver started to make a pot of tea. The fat man asked me if I wanted a cup, but I refused. I said, "I just want to go home." The fat man said, "You're not going home. There's no way you're getting out of this."'

After they had their tea break, they continued to beat him and made a half-hearted attempt to strangle him. But it was more by way of adding to the torture than a genuine attempt. They then produced a knife and started to cut the veins on his wrist with the intention, obviously, of killing him. When he was taken from that building, he was left for dead in a nearby entry off Carnan Street in the middle Shankill. The police were eventually tasked to the report of a body lying in the entry. An all-too-common occurrence in the area. They subsequently arrived and discovered that he was still alive. They had him taken to the Mater Hospital on the Crumlin Road. Due to the severity of the assault, myself and another detective, Roy Turner, were sent down to see to him in the Mater and check out the circumstances and his exact injuries.

He was in too bad a condition to even begin to speak to us and he had to remain in hospital for quite a number of days. We visited him regularly, even after he eventually had to be moved over to the Royal Victoria Hospital. We managed to build up something of a relationship with him, despite the horrendous torture and time that he had been put through.

When he got released from the RVH, Roy and I went over to collect him. He came back with us to Tennent Street, and we continued talking to him and asked him to stay in Tennent Street. We had an idea to see if we could identify the assailants. There was an election coming up in the Shankill area, so we knew the area around the road itself would be very busy. We decided we would take turns in the back of a police car and drive him round the Shankill area and see if he could identify any of the people who had assaulted him. He received a hell of a beating. He knew he was lucky to live to tell the tale, so he was keen to help. He agreed to come out in the car with Roy and I, with him in the back with a baseball cap and sunglasses on. We started off on Cliftonville Road where he had been picked up. To our surprise, he remembered exactly everywhere he had been taken in the back of this yellow Cortina. It was a very busy afternoon on the Shankill Road. We hadn't gone very far when he recognised someone from behind, and he just said, 'That fat bastard there. That's one of them.' It turned out to be Sam McAllister. We drove on down the road. There was a road traffic accident. He said, 'Those three guys' – they were watching the accident – 'the one in the light-coloured trousers, he's one of them.' I didn't know who he was, so I got on the police radio to the uniform cop who was dealing with the accident. I asked them to go over and ID the three guys watching the accident. Ironically, they were standing outside the doctor's surgery. I stressed they should make sure they got proper ID, which they did. He turned out to be Benny 'Pretty Boy' Edwards. We now had two of them.

We went back to the station to tell our detective inspector that two of the assailants had been positively identified. Very quickly it was decided that the arrangements should be made to have these guys arrested the next morning at six o'clock. When the detective inspector heard that Sam McAllister was one of the people named, he said that if McAllister was there, Billy Moore would have been there. 'Those two wouldn't go to the toilet without each other.' So arrangements were made to arrest Moore, a quick check of whom had shown that he had been stopped by police driving a yellow Ford Cortina with Sam McAllister on board as well. They were arrested the next morning [except Edwards who was arrested later] and taken to Castlereagh

Holding Centre for interview. Four knives were found in McAllister's house at the time of his arrest.

No one initially realised the significance of what they had just done, or the arrests they had just made. It would lead to the biggest trial in British legal history [which it remains at the time of writing]. The interviews ended up being very difficult matters, as they were experienced criminals who had trouble even admitting their names never mind the assault on Mr McLaverty. The interviews were like pulling teeth, despite the solid evidence against them for the kidnapping, torture and attempted murder of McLaverty.

During the torture of McLaverty, Sam McAllister had rolled up his sleeve to show a bullet hole in his arm, which he said happened defending Ulster from Fenians. During an interview, the police wanted to see his arm but he didn't want to show them. So the police assisted with the removal of his shirt, which is why in police photographs he is standing shirtless with his arms behind his back.

The bullet hole and tattoos were there, exactly as McLaverty had described – there was no doubt it was him. Given the sadistic nature of the assault, coupled with the knife wounds slashing the wrists, it became apparent there was a good chance that these guys may well have been the Shankill Butchers. They eventually admitted their part in the assault, but only after some very effective interviewing. With admissions made in the McLaverty case, they thought that they would get out after that and we had nothing else to put to them. Then their associates that were known to the police started to be arrested as well.

Billy Moore pleaded guilty to eleven murders and was convicted of a further eight. Judge O'Donnell said to Moore in court, 'You pleaded guilty to eleven murders carried out in a manner so cruel and revolting as to be beyond the comprehension of any normal human being. I am convinced that without you, many of the murders would have not have been committed.' When being led from the court, Moore waved and smiled at the spectators in the public gallery.

The McLaverty investigation was the beginning of the end for the Shankill Butchers. Their reign of terror was over. The advice of Detective Inspector Fitzsimons when Billy Moore was arrested was unquestionably a factor. And if it hadn't been for Gerry McLaverty's survival, dear knows how many other people might have died.

20:57 – CID Office, Belfast City Centre

It wasn't very hard to get yourself killed in Belfast back in those days. You could literally get killed or seriously injured just because of the side of the street you were walking on. It gave an indication as to what area you were going to, and therefore whether you were a Protestant or a Catholic.

One night behind the City Hall, there was a bit of a fight. This young lad was confronted as he made his way home by the 'other side', and was hit on the head. He went home and after a while he got more and more sleepy. He died during the night. It turned out he had a small prick round the side of his head, where one of the assailants had hit him with his belt. We assumed the point of the buckle punctured his skull, which then bled into his brain and the young lad died. So that started a murder investigation.

I decided to do a bit of undercover work and I dressed up like a tramp to move around Belfast, to see if I could see any of these gangs running about, because they wouldn't bother with a tramp. Around the City Hall, I was picking up butts and poking in the bins like a tramp would do. These bloody soldiers came along, and this solider wanted to know if I had any identification on me. Then he just took me by the scruff of the neck and pushed me up against the railings and kicked my feet apart. He then put his hands up my legs and felt up round my balls and gave me a squeeze. I said to him, 'Look, I'm a policeman.' He said, 'What?' I was able to smuggle out my warrant card and show it to him. I could have done him for assault. I'm not sure if it was the UDR or the regular army.

I worked for quite a while round the town trying to identify the gangs from both sides who were attacking people. Eventually we got a guy for the attack. He was done for manslaughter. He came from the Prod side in Sandy Row. There was actually quite a big inquiry into that one; the poor lad was only seventeen or eighteen. Terrible waste of life.

21:01 – Uniform Duties, Belfast City Centre

Going out on patrol in Belfast or indeed anywhere else in Northern Ireland always had its dangers. The only thing you could do, apart from rely on luck, was make yourself as difficult a target as possible. These people, despite the impression they like to give of themselves as heroic soldiers, would generally move on if they felt there was the slightest danger to them. The disturbing thing about that is you are really saying, 'Pick someone else. I'm too dangerous to you. Kill them instead.'

When you went out on foot patrol, or the beat as it's commonly known, there would always be at least two of you, so that you could cover each other in case of attack. That would be in a relatively 'safe' area. In the likes of west Belfast, you might have had the two cops on patrol and about twenty soldiers around them. It was all down to the scale of the threat.

Strictly speaking, you should really have stuck to opposite sides of the street to watch out for each other. The theory being that if one of you got attacked, the other one could return fire and call for help. The one thing this theory doesn't allow for is human nature. Sooner or later you would come together for some reason. It might be to discuss something, have a smoke or whatever. From the gunman's point of view, that is when you're vulnerable.

One of our supergrasses, a very dedicated terrorist who was in the INLA with a lot of kills under his belt, mentioned one such incident in his statement when he decided to turn and give evidence against his former colleagues. He said he had been out for a few drinks with his main partner in crime and when he got home he was bored. The two of them were probably the last of the roaming gunmen. In other words, they didn't worry about spending a lot of time planning a hit. They would just go and do it and find a suitable random target.

They decided to go out for a drive round the centre of Belfast to see if they could find any peelers walking about to have a shot at. There was a snooker tournament on in the Ulster Hall and two peelers had been put on the beat outside the hall to keep an eye on things. Anyway, they sat up the road from them in a car with a rifle and watched them for over an hour. They didn't come together once, and he said he didn't want to take the risk of the other one returning fire at him. Had they come together just once, for even a few seconds, they were both dead. There are probably quite a few policemen and soldiers alive today who will never know how lucky they are or how close they came to being dead.

21:03 – Uniform Patrol, West Belfast

An armed robbery had gone wrong. We got a report of armed men being seen on our patch. They had got into this house in Finaghy Road South to lie up for a while and let the heat die down, so they could make good their escape.

We, of course, didn't know this yet and were spread out – although we could always see each other – walking through the area, looking for anything wrong. Reports like this were quite common, but you didn't really expect them to still be around by the time you got there. Unless, of course, the call was a 'come on'.

One of the boys, John, had walked into the garden of this house and was just walking around when he saw a gunman inside. John was on his own but immediately started shouting, 'Police, police! Come out with your hands up!' while pointing his gun at the building. By a fluke, he had decided to dander up to the house the gunmen had decided to hole up in for a while. He kept shouting as loud as he could at them, but then started running round the building. He was going from the front of the house to the back. Then to the front again to make sure they didn't get out and make good their escape. All the while shouting at them to surrender. We actually got them. They came out with their hands on their heads just as other police were arriving. There were three of them. John had actually managed to surround a house on his own and arrest three armed terrorists. Which, when you think about it, is a pretty hard thing to do!

21:09 – Special Branch, Greater Belfast Area

An informant of mine was brought into a Sinn Féin advice centre to be 'interviewed' about his involvement in petty crime, or antisocial behaviour as the IRA called it. It was a fairly common occurrence in republican-controlled areas. In many ways it backfired on them. The young lads they were giving out punishment beatings to grew up hating them, and knew a lot of cops through their crimes. They also knew what was going on in their area just as well as the IRA did.

My source told me the local IRA commander, Terence 'Cleeky' Clarke, was doing most of the interviewing with a few other local IRA men helping. These were not gentle affairs by any means. Very soon they were giving him a bit of a beating while they questioned him. This went on for about forty-five minutes and then they put a gun in his mouth while he sat on the chair. He thought that was it. They were going to shoot him. But to his relief they resumed the torture and questioning with the gun still in his mouth. It would have been unlikely they would have killed him in the office. They would more likely take him somewhere else. Of course he didn't know that.

This went on for a while when into the room came Martin Meehan, a very senior and well-known republican from the area who had just been released from prison a few weeks earlier. Prior to prison, he had been the long-standing IRA commander in the area. He was very keen to re-establish his position and started to interfere with the interview. It became a contest between the two IRA men about who was in charge, with my man being the meat in the sandwich. Both men became very prominent members of Sinn Féin. Meehan told Clarke to back off and take the gun out of his mouth, as he was just a kid. Meehan was told to fuck off and an argument broke out between them. The argument became so heated, the two of them went outside to resolve it rather than do it in front of everyone.

As my man put it, 'I'm sitting there tied up with a gun in my mouth having already been beaten for ages. I'm shitting myself and these two fuckers are arguing about who's in charge. Eventually the two of them came back in, Meehan having prevailed. Clarke smashed me in the face with the gun, and said, "See all the trouble you've caused, you wee fucker?" He smashed me in the face again. The next thing that happened was I was then trailed out the back door by the other men and told to fuck off. I was convinced up to then that I was going to be killed. They just dumped me in the street. It was the worst day of my life. Who do those bastards think they are? I still have nightmares about it. But I was lucky, I survived."' When they interview people, the human rights they hold so dear in public do not apply. Incidentally, about six weeks later, Meehan was arrested for more terrorist offences and subsequently jailed again.

21:15 – Musgrave Street Police Station, Belfast City Centre

Vincent McCormick took a call one evening from a man who had decided to throw himself off the Europa Hotel. Vincent was the duty inspector in Musgrave Street. But your man was fairly determined and didn't want to talk to anybody. He was a Catholic fellow and had his mind made up as to what he was going to do. Vincent took off his shirt and turned it back to front, so it looked like he had a white collar on. He went up to the man and let on he was a priest. The man was none the wiser in the ever-fading light and eventually he talked the guy down. He just really needed someone to talk to who would listen to his problems and not judge.

21:21 – CID Office, Mountpottinger Police Station, East Belfast

Every now and again we used to have drink in the office, where we'd push all the tables together and get rid of all the files and have a bit of party. We would invite people over from other CID offices, maybe somebody had been transferred or something. It didn't really need a great excuse.

This night we all had been having a fairly good session. Craic was good, as it always is, and everybody was in very good spirits. The evening wore on and one of the boys got ready to go home. He rode quite a small motorbike at the time and I remember seeing him stumbling around in the office. He was walking round putting on his big coat, getting himself all buttoned up, scarf on. Then he went down to his desk and made sure the drawer was locked and put his crash helmet on. It was one of those full face ones with a visor at the front. He had his back to me and all I could see was him bobbling about and jerking round. I was wondering what the hell was wrong with him. But then he starting bobbling around in the chair, didn't say anything, didn't move. But he kept moving and jerking more and more quickly and violently. I went to see what was wrong with him. I turned him round to get a look at him. With his visor, I couldn't see his face at all. He'd actually been sick in the helmet, but he was so drunk he hadn't had the brains to undo the visor or indeed the helmet. He was jerking around because he couldn't breathe. If had been somewhere on his own he probably would have drowned. It was the funniest thing. I held him steady while they undid the visor, and the fluid just poured out. He looked stunned. I don't think he had realised what had happened to him, but fortunately he survived.

22:37 – CID Office, Downpatrick Police Station

My first encounter with the IRA was just after I joined in 1975 and was moved to Downpatrick. I was sent there because my father had died the year before. They moved me so I could live at home to help my mother, as I was single at the time. Normally single men were moved all over the place to the likes of the border. I was from Newcastle, so Downpatrick suited me. I was stationed there a fairly short time when I was seconded into CID. It was just about a year and a half into my police service, which was quite early on to get into CID.

There was a guy operating in the area named James Martin Hamill, who we knew was terrorising farmers and other people residing in outlying remote areas. The way his gang worked was to arrive, often during the night, smash their way in, tying the occupants up and robbing from their farmhouses. Quite often beating the people up, to terrorise them into telling them where they kept money, jewellery and valuables hidden. Special Branch had information that he was going to hit this house one night with his friends. We got into the combat clothing, got the Sterling [submachine gun], a couple of magazines of ammunition and flares, and off we went in the hope of catching them in the act.

We could feel the build-up to the whole thing as it was happening. Motorbikes were circling around this rural area, including the target farmhouse, which was out of keeping with the normal traffic of the area. We were lying in the field waiting and the next thing they actually came up behind us. We were lying at this tree in complete darkness, trying to remain still and make no noise. As they were passing us, one of the guys with me, Arthur Lusty, dropped a bit of the flare, which of course made a noise that in the circumstances sounded as loud as an earthquake. One of them turned round and said, 'What was that fucking noise there?' Then you could hear one saying, 'That's only Minty's oul' donkey.' Minty was the neighbour of the farmer they were going to rob. We decided we were going to have to go early. We were concerned for our own safety as we knew these people would be armed. So we fired the flares off. They started to run and we chased them down the field, threatening them as we ran to try and get them to stop. We arrested three of them, but James Martin Hamill got away and he was the main man.

He had been on the wanted list for quite a while

around Downpatrick. He used to come out of the Flying Horse housing estate and throw stones at the police cars patrolling the area, taunting them to try and get him. He really was making a fool of us to be truthful. I had moved into uniform again and I was out on patrol and there was information that he was coming in towards Downpatrick from Ardglass in a van, and he was heading towards the Flying Horse. We went up there and set up a roadblock. The van came along towards our checkpoint. They saw us and the van immediately screeched to a halt. They all got out and he took off on foot running into the Flying Horse. He was like an athlete. I went after him and started to chase him through the Flying Horse, which was quite a hostile republican estate. As I got further into the estate, all my colleagues were dropping off behind me. We were wearing body armour, which didn't help, but I was still maintaining the distance of about twenty yards from him. I couldn't get any closer but he couldn't any further away from me. Then the locals were starting to come out and I could see him throwing rings from his fingers. It turned out he was throwing stolen stuff away as he ran. I had my gun drawn. I shouted that I was going to shoot him. But he still didn't stop. He just went to go over a fence and I caught him up. I got him. I trailed him back through the housing estate with the gun at his head. When anybody else came near me, I pointed it at them until I got back to the police car. By that time the boys had caught up and came down to help. I had walked quite a bit through the estate with him, which was a danger in itself. We got him safely back to the station. I was feeling quite pleased with myself.

Two days later, I was returning home to Newcastle. I had been on a rare day off. Gillian and I had been shopping in Belfast that afternoon and we'd gone back to my house to get a bite to eat. I dropped her down to her home again.

As I was coming back up to my house to park, unknown to me, two gunmen were across the road waiting to murder me. I would suggest that was why I was targeted – because I had arrested Hamill. They fired something like twenty-eight shots at me. Thankfully I wasn't hit.

This was at my mother's house. I was closing the gate. As soon as I barred the gate, that was obviously the trigger for them to shoot. All hell broke loose. I heard a massive bang and the gravel beside me just scattered. I threw myself behind a hedge. I had my gun, my Walther pistol. But I may as well have had a water pistol. I actually thought to fire a couple of shots in the air and then it went quiet. 'Maybe they think they've got me,' I thought, but I was worried that they'd come over to finish me off. But they were making good their own escape. They were the biggest cowards. They were going in the other direction.

I thought, 'I'm not going to go to the house, because if they follow me they'll know I'm at the house.' I actually fell over a wall, which hurt my leg, and then went two houses away from mine to people who were Catholic neighbours and very good people. I rapped their back door with the gun pointed down the side of their driveway. I can tell you if anybody came around that corner they were getting it.

I had knocked their door, but the bullets had hit their house as well. They thought I was the gunman, trying to get into the house. My voice was distorted because of fear. Eventually they let me in, and I rang the police. I rang my brother Ken and I rang Gillian. Ken got Abe, my other brother, and they went out on the hunt for the gunmen. They had worked out what way they felt they would try to escape and went hoofing round the area to try to cut them off. Ken even brought a shotgun with him.

Gillian drove through a police roadblock to get to me. The police stopped her and said she couldn't go any further and she just drove through them. We laugh about that now. It turned out that one of the gunmen was actually a friend of mine from school. He is now dead. The IRA shot him because he was believed to be an informer. Ever since what happened that night, I could never go back home again. I had to sleep on settees, at Ken's house and Gillian's house. Then the police in their wisdom, when I went back to work, moved me to Killyleagh Police Station to sleep in it. I had to go in every night. I was the only one in it, there was nobody else.

I had to drive to Killyleagh, open up the big double gates of the police station. I felt I was in even more danger going in and out of there. It wasn't just the uniform they were after. They had me personally targeted as Dave Evans. It was an individual, it wasn't just a peeler. It wouldn't have taken them very long to work out if they followed me again to Killyleagh Station that it took time to open those big gates. It was quite a lonely, dangerous time.

Ken and I had to team up just to go back and visit our mum. We obviously wanted to help her, paint her house and do what we could for her. There was one day we had Ken on security with a shotgun and a pistol, while Abe and I were painting the house with pistols on us. It was a ridiculous situation, and the authorities couldn't have cared less. We even identified a car in a lay-by down the road. We took the number of it and it turned out to be owned by an IRA man. He obviously had spotted us and was watching our activities. It was very obvious we were ready for them because we just lay looking over the wall, keeping a watch up the road. To this day, when I go near Newcastle I still have to use false names. I was in the main street about three weeks ago. I booked a meal and I booked it under Gillian's maiden name. When I got into a taxi I had to book it under Gillian's name. I didn't want to use the name of Evans because there was still a dissident threat in Castlewellan. Almost thirty years later, I'm still having to think on my feet.

No police officer ever came to speak to me officially after the attack on me at the house. I never got a statement taken from me until about two years later, when a uniform sergeant came to take one that was in relation to a claim that I had put in for injuries. It was turned down because my injuries weren't serious enough. I think they awarded me about £300 for loss of earnings, with which I bought myself a Zanussi washing machine which only packed in last year.

22:38 – CID Office, York Road Police Station, North Belfast

I was in York Road in the CID. We got a call to attend an armed robbery at the Northern Bank in an industrial estate. The suspects were subsequently arrested and it turned out they were on the fringes, slightly more than sympathisers, of a republican terrorist organisation, let's say. One of the fellows involved had used his wife's car. The car led us to them. We had to interview his wife in relation to the robbery, as the car had been seen. We needed to know how he came to have her car. We arrested her for interview as well. During the course of the interview, it came to light that she worked for British Telecom in Belfast. Most peelers' phones were ex-directory, as were probably UDR members'. She was actually responsible for the allocating of ex-directory numbers and had full access. It's not hard to work out how terrorist groups were able to find out where members of the security forces were living.

22:39 – Castlereagh Holding Centre, East Belfast

The Shankill Butchers were a team of people who were

absolutely ruthless, sociopathic killers. I honestly believe that, because they grew up in Northern Ireland, they were able to hide behind the Troubles and use that as an excuse to kill. But they were so into killing and cruelty that I believe they would have ended up murderers no matter where they had been from. They would have found some reason for it. The Troubles here just gave them an excuse.

They had terrorised north Belfast generally and the Antrim Road area. The whole area was in such a grip of fear that people were scared to go out at night. They were charged with nineteen murders, although they killed many more, and as many Protestants as they did Catholics. In fact, one of the things that made them so difficult to catch would have been because they didn't really plan anything. There was no MO, as we'd call it – modus operandi. It was just random. Very often they would just take a feed of drink and then go out to kill a 'Taig', to use their own terminology.

They would just head off to an area where they assumed that if you were walking about you were going to be a Catholic. Anyone else who got in the way, well that was just tough luck. They would take you back to wherever they wanted to if they'd the time, and just torture people and kill them.

The first one of the Butchers to break was someone I had dealt with many many times. He had been in Castlereagh for interview loads of times. It was like a holiday home for them, or a home from home. They had been in and out so often. They would typically spend the seven days of their detention in complete silence, not utter a word and we would get nowhere with them. Others wouldn't shut up and would talk about anything under the sun except why they'd been arrested. But I suppose time moves on, and the blood lust starts to take its toll, no matter how tough or hard they think they are. 'Basher' Bates was the first one of them to go. He'd been brought in and hadn't been talking, just doing what he normally did. We really needed one to break, because witnesses weren't available. Nobody in the area would have dared say a word to the police or given information because they would have been killed as well, if they'd have been found out or even suspected of talking to the police.

Basher was in being interviewed and I can remember walking into the interview room. He was sitting at the wee table in the middle of the room and looked up and nodded his head to acknowledge me. He knew full well who I was and said, 'Hello.' I just looked at him and said, 'You're fucked this time, Basher.' He looked down and he said, 'I know.' He asked if he could speak to me on my own. The two other detectives got up and left the room. He asked, 'Would you go and tell the wife why I'm in?' I sensed something different about his manner and demeanour. There was something unusual about him but I didn't quite know what he was thinking or going to do. I actually said to him, 'Aye, I will.' I drove back over to Highfield estate and went to his house. His wife was there. She was a nice woman and she was actually very good-living. I think she was a Christian. I asked to speak to her and we went into the living room. She was obviously expecting very bad news or I wouldn't have been there. I sat her down and I told her what had happened and why Basher was in and what we were wanting to talk to him about.

She just immediately became hysterical while trying to take in what I had told her and then broke down. It was just disbelief. She couldn't understand how this could be right. She ended up fainting and we had to get an ambulance for her, to take her away. So it just shows you – people think somebody in the family must have known but I can assure you in this case she hadn't got a clue. She was as horrified as anyone else to find out what was going on.

I went back over to Castlereagh and I went in to Basher in the interview room. He said, 'Well, how did she take it?' I said, 'Basher, how the fuck do you think she took it? Not very well. She's very upset and all the rest of it.' He said, 'Right, that's it, she knows now. I just didn't want her finding out later.' He said he would make a statement about everything he was involved in. But he was only going to make it to me and true to his word that's exactly what he did.

He told us chapter and verse as to what his involvement had been with the cut-throat murders and named some of his accomplices. That obviously gave us stronger and more detailed information to take in and speak to the others about. Then in time the charges came from it and the convictions of the gang are a matter of record. It was such an awful time and the hate and fear that they brought out.

My only regret about the whole thing is that Lenny Murphy, the boss of the Butchers, was never convicted of any of the murders. He got into prison but he was even organising murders when he was in jail. I'm just sorry he never got convicted as he should have been for the Butcher murders. He ordered the killings to start again to shift suspicion away from himself, given he was in jail. When he got released from prison on firearms charges, he killed someone, I think on the first or second night, just to let everyone know he was back. Eventually he got his comeuppance, as they all do. It was by the IRA, because even the other loyalist paramilitaries were scared of him, although they wanted him out of the way just as much as anybody else did. He was shot dead in a mustard Rover car up in Forthriver Park, going to see his girlfriend. It was the IRA, as I say, but the reality of it is that the murder was set up by the UVF working with the Provos. They told them all the details they needed for the hit.

It was really just more politically correct to have republican terrorists kill him rather than for them [the UVF] to have killed him themselves. There might have been a big show at the funeral, but no tears were shed. It was like a weight being lifted off the backs of the people of that area when he went, and indeed when the others got arrested. They were the most horrendous, horrendous times; just awful people.

22:40 – My Dad

My father was a policeman. Just before I joined, I can remember going out for the evening, meeting up with some friends for a few beers. This must have been 1969. I arrived home with my long hair, feeling like a bit of a hippy. Quite pleased with myself, having had a few drinks, feeling all grown up. He obviously thought I was late home. It was probably as late as eleven o'clock at night. Of course nowadays people only go out at eleven. I tried to get the key into the door, at which point the door flew open. The Troubles had started, and of course people were worried about their kids being out, especially as we were living in Belfast. There he was; standing there at his full height. He looked at me as only a policeman can and said, 'What are you doing out at this time of night in the middle of an armed insurrection?'

22:43 – CID Office, Antrim Road Police Station, North Belfast

When I was in Antrim Road CID, I had the responsibility for Newtownabbey subdivision as well. There was a robbery of a post office delivery van, cash in transit. The security box with the money was taken. Two men held up the driver at gunpoint. They had to cut the chain which attached the security box to one of the delivery men.

I found a witness who had seen a car driving from the scene. I had another witness who'd seen two guys getting out of the same car, before running into a block of flats. He wasn't aware there had been a robbery, but he communicated that to us. We knew these were more than likely the culprits. The robbery had happened a relatively short distance away. They were in Rathcoole estate. We went along to the scene and the uniform guys were sealing this huge block of flats off. It wasn't practical to break down every door in the block, plus a lot of the residents were at work. I then went back to Newtownabbey Station, telephoned the post office security people, who made me aware that this box when it was deactivated was likely to produce a siren noise, which sprayed dye around the place, in tandem with this stinking smell. I got in touch by radio with the uniform people who were there and said to them, 'Can you listen at every door for this noise, and be aware that there should be a distinctive smell?' I went back immediately to see the Land Rovers disappearing. I think they had an urgent call-out or maybe they thought I was nuts wanting them to smell the whole block!

I waited there. I got in touch with a colleague who came along and systematically the two of us started at the ground floor and worked our way up, having a sniff through all the letter boxes as we went, and listening out for a particular sound. I was thinking if anyone sees us sniffing doors they'll phone the bloody police for us! We got to the seventh floor. I have a very bad sense of smell, but he said, 'There's a peculiar smell here.' Then he said, 'There are very few windows open in this whole block.' But one was open on that same floor. We got in touch with the DMSU and told them to come up and bring a door opener. We briefed them in the stairwell. They said, 'We'll break the door open.' I said, 'No, we'll knock the door first and then go in if there's no reply.' We duly knocked the door and there was no reply. We opened the door forcefully, and inside we find the cash box, the money, a load of guns. The place was covered in dye, with four purple men too, all of whom were arrested, taken to Castlereagh Holding Centre and subsequently convicted.

22:45 – Greater Belfast Area

There was a team from the UVF who had been carrying out murders – this would have been in the 1970s. They were approached by their commander and introduced to this guy who was a Catholic. He had come back from America to avenge the death of his brother. His brother was shot dead by the Provos, along with another man. He managed to make contact with the hierarchy of the UVF in the Shankill area. He actually joined a unit of the UVF, despite his being a Catholic from west Belfast. He told them he had been in the military in the States and had a proposition for them. He would murder Provos with their assistance, but he wanted to specify who they were to be. He targeted the ones who killed his brother and he murdered five of them, I think.

He killed the two main ones he was after. When he was trying to get another one, he was crawling through a field to this old shebeen, which he knew this boy would be coming out of at some point. Sorry, I shouldn't laugh but they always had security round these places. The Provos and the UVF always had security men outside round their clubs and meeting places. Your man was lying in the grass, waiting on one of his targets coming out of the club, when the security man came out to check round the premises and tripped over him. He dragged the security man to the ground and killed him. I'm told he strangled him on the spot, did the killings he had planned to do and that was him. He had been put up by the UVF in a club in the Woodvale area until he disappeared. He never came back or was heard of again. After he had satisfied himself that he had avenged his brother, he flew back to the States and effectively got away with it. No one has any idea who he was.

22:59 – Mobile Patrol, Malone Road, South Belfast

There was one incident that could be described as a comical death, though a death should never be described as comical, I suppose. I was in uniform on the Malone Road, where we were doing a road check on vehicles coming out of Belfast. I saw a Mini coming out of one of the side streets behind me with no lights on, and it started kangaroo hopping down the Malone Road. I stepped in front of it and put the red light from my torch on. The car came to a stop a few feet from me and stalled. I went up to the door and there was a big fat man sitting in the passenger seat with a Chinese meal on his tummy. The Chinese meal was all down his chest and he looked as if he was out cold. The driver, meanwhile, couldn't even bite his finger, he was absolutely full drunk.

I said to him, 'Is this your car, sir?' He couldn't even speak, so I said, 'I'm arresting you for drunk driving.' I put him in the back of the Land Rover and asked, 'Who's your passenger? I've got to get him home.' There was no way he was walking. Because he was huge, really big. So there was me and a couple of other policemen sorting it out, when the sergeant arrives on the scene. There was also a policeman in my section at the time who was a bit of a character, sort of like a hippy. This was about 1974. He had joined the police, but he loved the guitar. He also used to write poetry about things that happened in the station. This policeman was a peace lover and he should never have joined the police. He should have been a folk singer and gone to California. Somewhere like San Francisco would have suited him more.

He had arrived late for duty that night and he walked up to the scene of the roadblock because it was near to the station. I saw him talking to the boy in the back of the Land Rover, but I was too busy trying to deal with the passenger to pay much attention to him. I was looking in at him and thinking, 'How the devil am I getting him home?' Because when I'd asked the driver to tell me his address, he'd said to me, 'You're the fucking policeman, you find out.' The next thing I saw your man getting out of the back of the Land Rover and walking off up the Malone Road. I said to myself, fuck's sake, that's my prisoner walking up the road, so I ran up the road after him, shouting at the policeman concerned, 'What the fuck are you playing at?' 'He said you arrested him for being drunk and I don't think he's drunk.' I realised then that the officer was drunker than the boy I had lifted.

I got the hold of him anyway and took him back and said, 'Get you back in that Land Rover.' He said, 'But that policeman told me I could go home.' I said, 'I'm in charge of you. Now get into that Land Rover.' I went over to the sergeant to make arrangements that I should drive the Land Rover to the police office, while one of the other officers should drive the Mini with the big fat man.

We found out his address. He lived only a few streets down in the student area. We needed to pull in there and put him safely into the house. Easier said than done. He lived in the middle flat and there were about ten big student fellows all sitting on the ground floor, drinking and playing music. So I rapped their door and said, 'Hello, boys, do you know a man called Darren O'Neill?' 'Is Darren drunk again?' 'Darren is pissed, could you give me a wee hand in with him?' We started carrying him up the stairs when

133

Sergeant Wilkinson arrived and asked, 'What are you up to?' I said, 'We're taking this drunk in. We're going to leave him up to his flat, then we're going to head up to the office with the prisoner.'

He said, 'That man's not drunk.' I said, 'He's full.' He said, 'He's not, he's dead.' I said, 'I don't believe you.' He said, 'Get him to the hospital.' They radioed ahead to the hospital that they were bringing in a man that maybe had had a heart attack. He was still warm. I didn't even know how the sergeant knew he was dead. I was only a young fella. I'd never seen a dead body before. He just looked like a drunk out for the count. We carried him back out again to put him in the back of the Land Rover and just slid him in through the back doors and flew like mad down to the hospital. They hit him with the electric shock treatment, but he was gone. Do you know what he died of? The Chinese meal had a lump of gristle in it about three inches long and he choked on it.

It transpired he only had two relatives, an old aunty and uncle. I dealt with the sudden death and the uncle dealt with the family. I was at the flat that he lived in and there were paintings everywhere. There were sketches as well, but mostly oil paintings. The aunty said to me, 'We have no interest in the paintings – if you want to help yourself to some, you're very welcome.' I said, 'I'm sorry, I can't do that. As a police officer, you're not allowed to accept gifts.'

As it turns out he was Dan O'Neill. If you wanted to get a Dan O'Neill painting now you would need £40,000. I could have had a wall full of them, sketches and all. We took the driver in and he got done for drink driving.

Nights
23:00–07:00

23:02 – Source Meeting, Londonderry

I worked in Special Branch in Londonderry for a number of years earlier in my career. I got a phone call from a guy, who I knew had been charged with offences of fraud. Fraud wasn't really our thing, but I wanted to keep him on board. This guy ran about with people who would have been involved with cheque fraud and anything else they could get their hands on. He was a bad article. He was a crazy person, a very dangerous man. He wanted to meet me to give me information relating to a large fraud case. My sergeant warned me, 'Be very, very careful what you're doing there. Don't meet him at the pre-arranged spot that you have. I'll tell you where he'll be at a certain time and you just turn up.' I went up then with another policeman, who was my back-up man. We met this fella. He didn't expect us. It was out in the country. We were able to have a chat with him, and he started to give some very useful information. But then he insisted we go on to have a drink in the hotel, which we were wary about.

We went into the hotel and he very quickly started to buy doubles for us, like a man on a mission. I told the bar person quietly, 'Don't be giving me doubles. Just keep any drinks to the bare minimum.' I wanted to keep my wits about me. This guy took an awful lot of alcohol. He was well used to it. My back-up fella was a great help, announcing he had to go somewhere else, leaving me on my own. I remained in the man's company, because I was keen to keep in with him. It also would have looked bad if I'd left. During the course of the conversation, we fell out over somebody. He was trying to say to me, 'I felt very sorry about such and such a guy getting caught by the CID detectives and losing his job.' I said, 'Don't be talking nonsense. You know all about that. You were the one who gave the information about him, which was actually false.' So we had an argument, and the doorman got involved.

137

He came over and told your man to calm himself down. I had to check in back at base. I wanted to let them know where I was. I made a phone call about five o'clock and checked if there were any messages for me. I spoke to my detective sergeant, who was a different one from the man who had warned me about meeting this guy. Everything was fine, so I went back into your man's company.

The next thing I knew I was in a car. We were travelling at speed. There was a woman in the car. A man was driving, and I was sitting beside the man I had gone to meet. He was full drunk and I didn't know where the fuck I was. I couldn't focus on anything. I didn't know what was wrong with me. The next thing I knew, we were in a house. The woman was getting very agitated and annoyed. She was trying to get the guy to calm down. He had lost his temper with me again and he started shouting and roaring at me, 'You're a fucking RUC bastard.' He couldn't think of things bad enough to call me. One good thing I thought was I had my gun on me, which he obviously knew I carried. He then saw me check, putting my hand down to where my gun was. He grabbed me and pushed me back on to the settee. Then he pulled my gun off me. We struggled about a wee bit on the chair. I was in trouble, and didn't understand what was wrong with me. The woman intervened. She kept shouting at him, 'Get him out of here, get him out of here. Don't be shooting him in here.'

I realised I was in serious, serious trouble. Every time he punched me, I thought he was hitting me with a hatchet blade. I was completely away with it. I didn't know at the time what it was, but I knew it wasn't alcohol because the amount of alcohol I had drunk was minimal. It was now about a quarter to seven. I was aware of all that was going on around me, but I couldn't lift my arms. I couldn't physically do anything.

I was eventually able to persuade your man to calm himself down. Then he mentioned the detective sergeant who was a friend of mine and said, 'I hate that so-and-so.' He started to call him names as well. I said, 'Sure, we'll invite him over.' I was trying to make him think that I was happy there with him having a few drinks together. At this point there was no way I was going to take drink or anything else. What I was really doing was counting up the windows to work out if I could jump straight through to get out of there and survive. I could hear them whispering down at the front door. I was aware there were males at the doorway but I couldn't see who it was. The woman was constantly talking to people who were coming to the door.

The realisation that I was in really serious trouble kept hitting me in waves. But still I had no control over my arms or legs. I managed to persuade him about the sergeant. I said, 'Ring him. Get him to come over.' He said, 'Sure, I don't have his number.' I said, 'I do, I'll ring him.' But he said, 'No, give me the fucking number.' I called the number out and he dialled it. Lucky enough, when we got the sergeant on the phone, he started talking away to him. There was a bit of banter between the two of them, but the man was effing down the phone at him until he said, 'Your fucking mate's in a republican area and he's never coming out of it.' I could not see how I was ever going get out of this alive. I knew the man was crazy enough to kill me himself or to get others to do it.

I managed to persuade him to give me the phone to talk to the sergeant and invite him over to join us. All this time I was trying to reassure him that I was completely oblivious to what was going on. I think he was just away with it. Whatever action he was gonna take, he was gonna take, because, well, he was nuts. He was opportunistic. What he'd done to me, as I was able to work out later, was that he had put stuff into my drink which he used to inject into dogs to make them run faster. He had shown me the tablets in the bar. He had them in a wee matchbox.

Thankfully, I was able to get talking to the sergeant on the phone. I dropped my voice and said, 'Listen, I'm in trouble. You've got to get me out of here.' He asked me where I was. I said, 'I'm in a house in the town and it's a republican area, that's all I know.' He said, 'Look for an address. Whatever you do, get an address.' I knew this conversation wasn't going to last very long. Your man was struggling with this girlfriend or whoever the woman was in the flat. She was really agitated about what was going on. I saw there was a pile of envelopes sitting beside the phone. The same address was on several of the envelopes. I said the address to my sergeant.

Next thing I knew, I was trailed down the hall out on to the landing. I struggled and fought with the people who had come in. I thought I was going to my death. I didn't even recognise the men. They were actually detective friends of mine, men that had known me for years. I didn't recognise them. I thought I had escaped at one stage. I ran and dropped down to the ground, thinking I'd hid. I'd actually only ran about three or four feet. I was on the landing. I put my hands up over my head. They picked me up, dragged me down a pile of steps and tossed me into the back of a vehicle. I thought, 'This is it. This is how it's going to end.'

I have very little recollection of what went on. I know now I was taken from there back to my own police division. Then I was brought home. When I arrived at my house, my wife answered the door to a fella who had driven me home. He hurried back up the path after propping me up on the door, and ringing the bell. I think he didn't want to be told off for me being in such a state. My wife said she saw me and realised right away there's no way this was alcohol. I went completely off the rails in the house. I was punching the doors and stuff. I thought I was shooting people with my right hand with nothing in it. My son was only about five. He had come down from the upstairs bedroom. I got him by the neck and held him to me, trying to get out of the room with him. The wife got her mum and dad to come to the house to help her. When I saw them, apparently I burst into tears, I must have thought when I saw them I was safe. I realised I was in my own house.

I had to go the next morning to watch a bail application, so I got myself sorted and went down in the car. I got as far as passing an army barracks when I had a flashback of what occurred the night before. I was back to square one. I didn't know where I was. I went to the bail application, then had to report over to the head of the area about all that had happened. He believed that I had gone out and got drunk and went with this guy willingly to this place. To say that he ate the ass off me would be the understatement of the year. I have a great respect for that man, always did. Great officer and absolutely backed you 100 per cent. But he literally tore me to pieces and I wasn't allowed to speak. I tried to a couple of times, but he told me to shut up and said I would be on the dole queue before he was finished.

I went over to my own area again and I met with a chief inspector and inspector who were waiting on me. They said, 'What on earth happened to you yesterday?' I told them as best I could. I raised the fact that I had asked for back-up to go and meet this guy. But they didn't have any due to overtime restrictions, so I had ended up going with that one guy – who I had never let on had left me to my own devices. So I survived.

That same person who brought me to the house had made a phone call to a police officer that he knew who was also in the Branch. He told him that he had a drunk Branch man up in his address and asked him to come and get me. When he made that phone call, I'd already been rescued from the house. He had made the phone call trying to let on that I was drunk and still in the place to muddy the waters and make him look better.

I found out later there was a strong likelihood it was his girlfriend was with him. Her son and his friends were all members of an extremely militant group of republicans. I have no doubt but for the work of my colleagues I was never coming out of there alive. I must say I think it contributed an awful lot to the post-traumatic stress which I eventually ended up suffering very badly from.

23:09 – Donegall Pass Police Station, South Belfast

In the early 1970s, I was stationed in Donegall Pass. Bombs were going off in the city all over the place. Uniformed officers were tasked to travel around in a 'bomb transit'. The transit went to bomb scares to free the police patrol cars and beat men to deal with ordinary calls. One day I was on the transit, I was left at Smithfield, and two or three others were sent down to Donegall Street to the *Irish News* office. Another scare came through to Castle Street, a big department store on the corner. Then another around the Albert Clock. It ended up we were leaving only one policeman at each site. We weren't exactly trained for it, either. We would guess if there was a bomb in a car by how low the rear suspension was. Or by going up to the suspect vehicle and smelling it. The explosives of the day smelt like marzipan. That's what you were smelling for.

Probably the most infamous day was Bloody Friday, when the IRA detonated more than twenty bombs over the city centre within a very short period of time. When the Oxford Street bomb went off, nine people were killed, and one hundred or so injured or maimed, some very badly. The bombs went off without warning. I remember going around to Oxford Street. Two women came up to me in the street asking me, 'Where will we go? Where will we go?' I didn't know where to direct them, because I didn't know where the next bomb was going to be. I sent them round to Musgrave Street Police Station, just to tell them something. But I didn't really know if it was safe.

When we got to Oxford Street, I saw this woman. I can't even tell you what she looked like because there was no way of knowing. I'm guessing she was a middle-aged woman. She had her back up against the wall and she quite literally had lost her chin, the bottom half of her face. She was standing there against the wall, no other marks on her. She was gurgling and squealing, trying to breathe with her chin sliced off. I tried to get her stuck back together as best I could. I was holding pieces in and tried to bandage it in a very primitive way to get the pieces to where they should be until I could get one of the ambulance men, who were dealing with other casualties.

Sirens were going all over the place. No one knew what was going on. After I got her wrapped up as best I could, I went to the site of where the bomb had actually gone off. Bits and pieces of flesh were all over the place. It was bizarre, like something out of a weird film set or dream. One soldier was just barely alive. A couple of soldiers beside him were dead, and very badly blown apart. Someone came into the station later with a soldier's foot in a plastic bag. That was days and days after it.

One policeman and I were picking up bits and pieces of bodies and placing them into plastic bags. There were body parts of a man under a car. I think he had been leaning on the car when the bomb it contained went off. On his torso was an Ulsterbus grey uniform. We picked up the torso and put it in a plastic bag. It was only when we went round to Musgrave Street Police Station later that we found out it was the other policeman's brother. He had helped me pull the torso out from the car of his own brother. He hadn't even recognised him. Although there was nothing much to recognise. It was just a trunk, the leg and shins. I mean, it's just beyond comprehension. The IRA planted the bombs. We know who organised it, but I suppose I better not say here. He's a well-known figure now in Northern Ireland life. It's one of those days that just sticks with you, the carnage. It's something no one should have to experience.

23:15 – CID Office, Strand Road Police Station, Londonderry

There has been much talk in the media about an improvement in relations between the Garda and the PSNI. I always found in the RUC, especially when I was up in Derry, that there was good contact and good relations between the two forces. For example, I had friends who lived in Eglantine in Derry and they moved to live in County Donegal in the Irish Republic. I was invited to visit them, but because of being stationed in Derry, and obvious security concerns, I was reluctant to go. I contacted the Garda close to Moville, and talked to the sergeant there. He said he would look after it. I gave him the day and the time of the planned visit. He said, 'You'll not be too long into the south until there'll be a car pull in behind you.' But he said, 'It will be unmarked and it will follow you to your destination. It will be a discreet distance away while you are there.' I thanked him and said, 'I'll try and not be too long.' He said, 'Be as long as you want.'

Sure enough, I wasn't too far into the Republic of Ireland when this car did pull in behind me with two men in it. They were in civilian clothes and I was happy enough. This is what the arrangement had been. My wife and I and the two kids made our way to our friends' house and parked outside. The Garda parked just a short distance up the road. They had a clear view of my car, the house and the surrounding area. We were in the house for about two and a half hours. When we came out, the two men were still there. My wife and I, along with the two children, got into our car and headed back towards Northern Ireland. About half a mile from the border, I got two flashes of the lights from the men behind and they pulled off. That was good cooperation. This was when there was allegedly no cooperation.

23:16 – Musgrave Street Police Station, Belfast City Centre

I went for a pint one night with another guy I worked with in CID in Belfast. When we got to the bar, two SOCO guys were there. They are the fellows who would come to the scene of serious crimes and gather up all the forensic evidence. In those days in Belfast, there were a lot of murders. We got talking to them, and as inevitably happens with cops, we started talking about work. It turned out there'd been someone found in the hills just outside Belfast. The body had been there for a while. It was a gruesome scene. As was unfortunately the way all too often, the drink came into play afterwards. They'd gone for a few beers to try to get what they had seen out of their heads.

One of them, Geordie, said, 'I just can't get the smell of that out of my head. It's desperate,' and he carried on drinking. He even switched drink to whiskey to see if that was any better. They were getting fairly tanked. He said, 'No, it's not working. I need to take another drink. I can still smell that. What is wrong with me?' It was only later on he discovered he had part of the brain of the person stuck on the sleeve of his jacket. So every time he took a drink he was getting the smell. Mind you, he got fairly drunk while he was working that out. That's the sort of thing the guys ended up laughing at. I still think it's quite funny. But that's just the black humour. I suppose it's a safety net for the people who have to attend these things. They find things funny that other people would be horrified at.

23:17 – Interview Room, Musgrave Street Police Station, Belfast City Centre

Car theft was always a big problem in Belfast. They were being stolen in their hundreds. The main supplier of 'drivers' was west Belfast. That's where most of them would end up, usually burnt out or wrecked. It got so bad the police ended up forming a squad to deal specifically with the so-called 'joyriders'. Or 'taking and driving away', to give it its real name. I worked in one of the teams. I must say it was very effective in reducing the problem. Some of them were pretty hardened criminals who had grown up in a tough area and were difficult people to interview. I was interviewing a very experienced joyrider one day about a large number of cars. I wasn't getting too far with him. I decided to change tack. A good mate of his had been killed in a stolen car a few days earlier. The car had been speeding around west Belfast when the driver lost control. The car crashed on a road that was lined with large mature trees. The car hit the tree head on. His friend had been in the back seat. His head went straight through the sunroof. The rest of him, however, did not. His head landed quite a distance from the car on some grassland. The metal edge of the sun roof had removed his head like an axe. It was pretty grim.

I had copies of the photographs that were taken at the scene by the police investigating. This included one of his friend's head lying on the grass. I showed this guy the photograph by dramatically throwing it on to the table to try and jolt him into seeing the error of his ways. He just looked at the picture, and then said, 'No wonder they fucking crashed. He was driving with his eyes shut.' That's what you were up against. They didn't give a shit about anything.

23:30 – Hastings Street Police Station, West Belfast
When I was based in Hastings Street, the army were stationed in North Howard Street Mill. Conditions there were pretty savage. On a six-month tour of duty, these young guys didn't get a chance to socialise or unwind at all. On one occasion, we [the police] suggested we have a cockroach race. The place was infested with cockroaches, so we'd no shortage of runners. It was just to try and break the monotony for the troops. Someone got the job of building this little obstacle course for cockroaches to race round. The army officers had their cockroach, and the RUC had their cockroach. This took place in the sergeant's mess, over lashings of drink, which we managed to smuggle in. It was like something out of an old black-and-white POW film. A good time was had by all. The regiment was the Black Watch. The officers won, but we felt there should have been an inquiry, as we suspected they'd been practising before the main event – because they supplied the cockroaches!

23:41 – CID Office, Belfast City Centre
I was on night duty when there were six bombings in one night. The IRA were having a big campaign across the Province, planting incendiary devices in the shops. They were cheap and easy to make, yet could cause millions of pounds' worth of damage.

As soon as you got to one, you were getting reports of another one somewhere else. The ATOs [ammunition technical officers] were running about like headless chickens. Imagine nowadays, six bombs going off in one night. The last one was in a baby store. They were going into clothes shops and putting them into the pockets of jackets. Staff of course had to stay on after work to search premises before they went home. It was quite a job. They were only the size of a packet of cigarettes, which in a big department store was hard to find.

Paint shops were always popular, because the paint was so flammable. I remember a couple of girls were going to plant one whenever I was in Woodburn Station in west Belfast. It was pretty much the norm to use girls. It was a loyalist paramilitary job this one. They were going to put incendiary devices in some of the stores up around Andersonstown. It was the loyalists' way of hitting back, to place the devices in a Catholic area. The UVF had given them £70 to go and do a bit of shopping and then plant these devices. It was one of the big new malls that had opened round there. When they came into the shop, one of the devices went off in one of the girls' coats. She started screaming and then her coat caught fire. The whole disaster was recorded on CCTV. They were caught very quickly.

The city centre was sealed off with security gates before long and civilian searchers checked people going into the city. There were searchers on the doors to the shops as well. But you could buy everything you needed to make an incendiary device inside the barriers!

23:44 – Waterside Police Station, Londonderry

There were some very sad times, tragic times. A friend was stationed with me in Waterside up in Derry. He grew up in Andersonstown, a very strong republican area in west Belfast. He was only twenty years of age. His father was dead, but his mother was alive and she still lived in Andersonstown. He hadn't been home for a long time, but decided he would go home the next time he was off and visit his mother. He didn't have a car, so he went out and bought a car for the trip back. It was a Lada. He bought it brand new. He was the butt of a lot of jokes from the boys in the station for buying a Lada.

People advised him to be careful during the trip. Some, including me, suggested maybe arranging to meet his mum somewhere else. He said, 'Look, I know they're bad, but they're not that bad.' The boys that would be sent out to get him were the boys he probably went to school with. He arrived up there on the Friday. Monday morning, he was out at the new car, dipping it for oil, checking it for water, getting ready for the long drive back to Derry. A car drove up. Two bullets in the back of the head. That was him.

23:45 – CID Office, Tennent Street Police Station, North Belfast

I was working in CID in Belfast in the 1970s. There weren't that many detectives. The force had to grow very quickly, as the Troubles took hold. It was a steep learning curve for the police. You barely had time to get the person's name and address before you were going to the next one. But we did what we could. Everything was investigated as best we could in the time available and with the manpower we had.

At one stage, I was in charge of lifts, arranging the arrest of people for terrorist offences, who had to be brought over to Castlereagh Holding Centre for interview. All terrorist suspects from the east of the Province were brought to Castlereagh, which became sort of famous or infamous, in no small part because of the organised complaints made by suspects regarding their treatment in custody. You'd try and organise a number of arrests at the same time. If it was about one major crime with several people involved, you might have wanted teams of interviewers organised.

On this occasion, we were looking for a fella for murder. During the loyalist workers' strike, there was a garage on the Crumlin Road that had stayed open. The UVF decided that this was a crime. They weren't being supportive of the strike. To take revenge, they decided to bomb it. There was a person sent to blow the garage up and to put other people off breaking strikes. Forcing their will on the community.

The person planted his bomb, which went off. Sadly, when it exploded, a member of the Ulster Defence Regiment had just pulled in to the garage to get petrol. He was murdered when the bomb went off. It would have been a nationalist-owned garage, which added to their interest in blowing it up. But a UDR man would not have been an intended target for loyalist paramilitaries. We got intelligence in about the person who had carried out the crime. A fairly good description and a name. He actually had been on the reserve list, in case we didn't get the ones from the other list of people we were after. He would have been arrested in due course. One of the people we had arrested admitted his crimes very quickly, so he was being charged and taken to court. Which meant we now had a vacancy and a spare team of interviewers. I know it sounds a very peculiar expression now, but that's the way it worked. I was over in Castlereagh, and I hadn't brought the sheet with all his details with me. I had left it at the station, but I was sure I could remember enough of the details to arrange to get him arrested.

I phoned the night man in CID to coordinate the arrest (these were normally done about 6 a.m.) to get him brought over to Castlereagh for interview. I told him who I was after, and where he lived. Well, they went out and arrested the man and brought him in for questioning. He was seen by a doctor, which was the procedure in those days, because of complaints alleging assault or ill treatment. They were seen by a doctor before they were interviewed and again prior to their release to show that they went out in the same condition in which they came in. He was brought upstairs to the interview room from his cell by uniform police, where two detectives were going to be interviewing him. They were interviewing him for about an hour or so, and decided that this wasn't him, he didn't do it. He was genuine enough with his answers, and these detectives weren't slow, they were very experienced and could tell very quickly that he didn't fit. The description wasn't quite right. The name was right, but they felt that his protestations of innocence were genuine.

They came to see me to tell me. I had another look at the arrest sheet as they were telling me. It turned out that with me not having the paperwork, they had arrested a person of the right name and address. But unknown to us, the father had the exact same name as the son. We had no reason to hold the father, so we had to arrange for his release, and organise a doctor to come in to see him before he could go. In the meantime, I told them to find the son and get him in here, so hopefully he didn't find out what we wanted him for. In other words, keep the father until you find and arrest the son. He was put back in the cell to await the arrival of the doctor.

When he had been examined by the doctor, I went down to see him to explain it was a bit of a cock-up on our part. I told him I was sorry about that and we were going to release him and offer him a lift home. He said, 'There is something actually I want to get off my chest.' He continued, 'Those two men interviewing me earlier made me think. That's all I've done since I was put back in the cell. There is something that's been worrying me for quite a few years now.' I asked, 'What's that?' He said, 'I was involved in planting the bomb at McGurk's Bar.' I could hardly believe what he was telling me. I arranged immediately for some detectives to take him back to the interview room while he was in the mood to talk, and see could they get a confession from him. He was brought in to the room, cautioned and the interview began. It turned out that indeed he had been involved, and maintained that he had had a terrible conscience about it since it happened. There were fifteen people killed in that explosion, and seventeen people injured. It had been playing on his mind, he couldn't sleep, bad dreams – the usual things. It's not that uncommon, although it is more irregular for them to want to confess their sins.

He told of his part driving the bomb to the bar where it exploded. It had been in a suitcase. There has been all sorts of subsequent speculation about this bombing. All sorts of ill-informed conspiracy theories. But I can assure you, this man had never come under police notice. There was no intelligence file about him. In any case, he said it had been bothering him and he had decided to admit his part. Although no matter how hard he was pushed, he refused, probably through fear, to name anyone else who was involved. Indeed, he went to his grave having served his sentence without ever naming anyone else. He remains to this day the only person convicted of it. He was Robert James Campbell, or Jimmy, as he was known. He was convicted in about 1978 for fifteen murders and seventeen attempted murders. The court recommended he serve at least twenty years in prison. Once he started talking, he also admitted shooting dead a Catholic workman in a van in Belfast, which he was also convicted of.

Of course we still had the son in custody about the bomb in the garage. Whilst the father admitted things fairly quickly, because his conscience had already been bothering him, it took a full seven days of interviews with the son to get him to see the error of his ways. But he eventually made a statement admitting his part in the bombing. He was subsequently convicted and sentenced. I always sort of put that down as a bit of a cock-up on my part about the name and not having the date of birth. But that was the day I cleared fifteen murders by mistake! It was just an indication of this job, you just never knew what was around the corner. I'm just sorry we didn't get the rest of the team.

Many years later the Police Ombudsman investigated the McGurk's bombing. I contacted the Ombudsman's office when their report came out and they asked me what I wanted. I explained that I wanted to help – that I could tell them what had happened because I was there. The report said that there was prior intelligence about this crime and that nothing was done about it. I told them that I was there, involved in the investigation, and I assured them about what happened – that there was no intelligence about this person. He hadn't come on to the radar at all. I also told them how he came to be convicted – that there was no sitting on anything; that it took place exactly as I have described to you, as the result of a mistake – but I have to say that the Ombudsman people were no more interested in listening to me than flying to the moon.

23:57 – Uniform Patrol, Shankill Road, West Belfast

I used to work in north Belfast, parts of which were like a war zone. One night, we were driving down the Shankill. I saw this crowd milling around outside one of the clubs, all looking in the one direction. It was just after closing time. We stopped to see what they were all finding so interesting. There was a lot of shouting and pushing going on amongst them. I got out and walked into the crowd. As I was pushing through them, they start telling me, 'It's all right boss, it's all right.' Further into the crowd, I could see a guy up against the wall, who seemed to be the centre of the crowd's attention. This guy's face was bright purple and he was up on his tiptoes, his hands straight down by his sides. His eyes looked as if they were about to come flying out of their sockets. There had been a fight inside. He'd had his throat cut with a bottle. They were trying to help him, but didn't want the police involved. All the 'plumbing' in his throat was exposed. A surgeon could not have removed the skin any tidier without severing something important. It was unbelievable. In that respect, he was lucky. His main problem at this stage was the first aid his mates were giving him. When I got to him, his face had got brighter. It turned out they had got a smelly old bar towel and were using it as a tourniquet on his throat. Instead of helping him, they were actually strangling him!

23:59 – New Barnsley Police Station, West Belfast

When I was promoted to sergeant, I was returned to uniform duties and posted to New Barnsley Station. This was during the hunger strike in 1981. The station was under some form of attack almost nightly and by very large crowds. We were surrounded by republican estates. Crowds also came across to New Barnsley from the Ballymurphy estate, just to attack the station. These were very difficult times indeed.

A much-favoured form of attack by the IRA on the station was the use of what were known as proxy bombs. The driver of a lorry would have a device placed in his vehicle and he would be told under threat where to drive to and abandon it. Which also ruled out any risk to the IRA.

There were only two sergeants at the station, myself and another guy, Sergeant Harry Montgomery. A lot of the men were more terrified of Sergeant Montgomery than they were of the IRA. A young reserve constable joined the station, and he was very much in awe of the sergeant.

He was also very perturbed about these proxy bombs. One day, he was on duty in the sanger at the front gate. A lorry came along and the driver jumped out and shouted, 'There's a bomb on board. I've been told to deliver it to the station.' The reserve constable cocked his weapon and said, 'Move the vehicle now.' The driver said, 'I'm not moving it. There's a bomb on board.' The reserve man said, 'Okay then, I'm gonna shoot you.' The guy got in and drove the lorry to wasteground in double time. Eventually the army technical officer came and defused the thing. I spoke to the reserve constable and said, 'What were you going to do, really?' He said, 'I was going to shoot him.'

You could make up your own mind whether the driver of the lorry was innocent or not. But with the mood that reserve constable was in, I think he was pretty lucky to escape with his life. I certainly believed him.

00:02 – Cookstown Police Station, County Tyrone

Loyalist paramilitaries had these 'romper rooms', where they beat up and interrogated their own side for crimes against the community or something. One time a very famous UVF boy was being interviewed by us. He said, 'You fellows think you can interview? I can tell you, when they've a red-hot poker up their arse, they fairly squeal.'

00:07 – Hastings Street Police Station, West Belfast

I was in Hastings Street. The IRA fired an RPG-7 Rocket at the station. It went into the canteen on the top floor and the only person injured was the new crime prevention man. That was his first day's duty. The irony of this was not lost on our black sense of humour.

00:09 – Uniform Patrol, Markets Area, Belfast City Centre

The murder of Constable Johnston Beacom occurred in,

of all places, Friendly Street in the Markets area of Belfast. We were driving down Castle Street when we heard the explosion. Then all the people in Castle Street cheered. We drove round by the Markets. Tommy was getting led by Davy up to the Land Rover. He had half of his friend Johnston Beacom's insides stuck to his flak jacket. Tommy was grey, dazed. He was in shock. We took him over to the Royal Victoria Hospital and got him sorted out. That's a night I'll never forget. The night the explosion went off killing a police officer, and everybody cheered. It's sick.

00:11 – CID Office, Donegall Pass Police Station, South Belfast

I wasn't long into the CID in Donegall Pass and Eddie Morgan, he was my mentor. We called up to the Wellington Park Hotel one night for a drink. We got a call over the radio to say there were firebombs around the city. One was reported to be in the Wellington Park. I informed the radio controller we would take the call to check out the hotel.

In about ten minutes, I was able to report that the firebomb had been located. I knew because my friend Eddie was sitting in a chair at the hotel, like a phoenix with flames coming up round him. He was sitting in the seat the firebomb had been planted in. He was a very lucky man. He didn't get burnt at all. But I'll remember the expression on his face until the day I die. It still makes me laugh thinking about it.

00:41 – The Job

It's funny when you look back over your career in the police. You just thought you were getting on with the job, that nothing affected you. You dealt with it and you moved on to the next thing. I remember going over to the British Open at St Andrews, I think it was 1984, with two detective friends. We had gone over for the weekend, to get a bit of a break. We drove over and we were enjoying the golf and having a few beers at night. I had never been to such a big golf tournament. I was just enjoying walking round with the crowd, switching off. I was walking up the side of the eighteenth at St Andrews, going along the pathway between the houses and the fairway, whenI heard the crowd start to shout. I then saw a man in uniform point. Panicking people were scattering. I instinctively hit the ground and was reaching round for a gun, which wasn't there. The next thing this golf ball landed, and rolled up the path beside me. I had to get up and rather sheepishly walk away. I felt like a bit of a twit. But it just shows you what way your mind was set.

00:47 – CID Office, Belfast

A lot of criminals over the years develop a great respect for some of the detectives who deal with them. I always found the detectives to be fair. Sometimes they could be quite brutal and harsh with these guys. But there was a respect from the criminal that the guy was doing his job. Quite often they would develop a reputation. One particular detective sergeant, who was a very dear friend of mine, would have had such a reputation. He was very well-known even within the force, never mind with criminals. I was interviewing a guy one day with another sergeant. We'd been getting nowhere with him. The fellow wouldn't speak to us at all. He was lying on the ground, doing handstands, anything to break up the flow. After you'd been speaking to these people for a while, you needed to step out of the room for a minute or two. Just to get your head showered, stretch and regroup. I was doing just that, and this sergeant I'm speaking of came along. He said, 'Who have you in?' I told him and he said, 'I know him. How are you getting on with him?' I said,

'He doesn't want to know us.' He said, 'Where is he?' and I said, 'In there.' He opened the door and walked in. Now this person hadn't spoken to us at all for a day. As in not even, 'Hello.' Not a single word had he uttered. But when I walked into the room again, he stood up and said, 'Hello, Mr Graham,' to my colleague. I just said, 'Look, I'll leave you to it.' I went back out. Sergeant Graham came back out no more than a few minutes later and said, 'He'll make a statement to you now.' I think that was a good example of the respect or maybe fear that this guy had for the sergeant. But it certainly worked. You felt like a bit of a twit because you couldn't do it. But that was experience that he had built up over the years.

00:50 – Crime Squad, Supergrass Interview

I interviewed Harry Kirkpatrick, who was second in command of the INLA. Harry decided to admit to all his involvement in terrorism. He asked me if I wanted to know his rank and I told him to go ahead. He said, 'I'm brigade adjutant, brigade quartermaster and brigade operations officer for the north.' I said, 'That's very good. I'm a detective constable, and that's the best you're getting.'

I told him to start at the beginning. He admitted shooting Hugh McGinn dead. He also admitted another five or six murders where he was present, but he didn't actually put the bullets in the people. Maybe he'd seen a reaction in me when he admitted murdering Hugh McGinn.

I said, 'If you're brigade quartermaster, you'll know where there's a weapon or weapons. So why don't you put a weapon on the table as a sign of good faith, and a sign that you're being truthful?' He said, 'Once I've been brought into custody, weapons on the outside will be shifted about. Just in case somebody admits anything.' I said, 'Come off it. There's no way in the wild world they will all be moved.

You're bound to know if you're brigade quartermaster where there are weapons.'

'All right,' he said, 'a Ruger rifle – will that do you? The main cathedral in Armagh, there's a Ruger rifle in it.' I said, 'Come off it, you're stalling. You know perfectly well that if I have to go and search a cathedral, I'm going to have some difficulty in getting a warrant.' He said, 'I swear to you, it's in there.' I got him to draw a map showing the organ. He said it was in there. We rang Armagh and got the search organised. They contacted an inspector in the middle of the night, who had great local knowledge of the area. He got a warrant. We went down early in the morning, got talking to the man that looks after the place, told him we had to carry a search out. Of course he contacted Cardinal O'Fee. The cardinal arrived at the scene very quickly. He was very cross. He said he was going to get straight on to the chief constable, saying this was ridiculous. The inspector explained to him that we had good and solid information, and we knew what we were looking for. Cardinal O'Fee realised the sense in what the inspector told him, and reluctantly said go ahead. He went straight to the spot and it was in the organ case just where Kirkpatrick said it would be. I remember being so relieved to see an evidence bag coming in to Castlereagh with the rifle in it.

01:06 – Special Branch Office, Belfast

It's no secret in Northern Ireland that paramilitary organisations on both sides of the divide ran their areas with an iron fist, dishing out their own form of justice for misdemeanours, perceived or otherwise. These punishments took many forms, from beatings, getting shot in the knees, expelled from the country, to being shot dead.

One of the paramilitary groups had been having an inquiry

into some missing funds from one of their clubs. These clubs were used by them for meetings and fundraising. Many a person's fate was decided in them. After one such meeting, it was decided in their 'court' who was responsible for taking the money. One of them was given the task of disciplining the guilty party. The person appointed to deal with the matter, and who phoned the fella concerned, was actually a good friend of his. He told him they had to discipline someone, and asked him to meet him in a flat off the Woodvale Road. He asked him to collect a gun and bring it with him. The person concerned turned up at the flat, and he and his mate sat down and had a bit of a chat. He was even given a can of beer while they were talking. He was sitting in an armchair, enjoying his drink, talking away to his friend and eventually he asked, 'Who's in trouble then?' As his good friend walked round the back of the chair, he just said, 'You,' and shot him in the head, killing him instantly.

01:07 – Uniform Patrol, Belfast

Punishment shootings happened all the time in Belfast. Still do, I suppose. The vast majority were by appointment. The victim would be told when and where to turn up, and would generally be shot by someone they knew. That's why they were rarely badly hurt. Most got shot in the fleshy part of the leg, rather than the actual kneecap. Others were very bad. The Prods did some in the early days with Black and Decker drills, which must have been as sore as it gets. But it was the strange sense of acceptance some of them had which amused me. I remember the first time I went to one, and noticing this guy had his trouser leg rolled up. While we were waiting for the ambulance, I asked him about the rolled-up trouser leg. He said, 'New pair of jeans, mate. Didn't want to get a hole in them!' That's Belfast for you. You can shoot me, but be careful with the jeans!

01:09 – Uniform Patrol, Riot, North Belfast

Riots in Belfast could carry on for days, and a lot of lives were lost, and a lot of people injured. One night during rioting, we [the crew of a Land Rover] decided to make an arrest. A large number of police were deployed in the area. Sometimes you would notice an obvious ringleader in the crowd, and move to get him off the street, which would also encourage others to disperse. We were a four-man crew. I was in the back with another fella. There was a bit of a lull in festivities, so we decided to go for this guy. We pulled up alongside him. One of the boys got out the front passenger door, and I got out the back to sort of get him between us. As the other fella grabbed him, and I moved to help, a huge crowd came from nowhere and attacked us. Bricks and bottles were landing all around us. One of the fuckers actually hit Larry on the head with an iron bar. He had an FRG [federal riot gun, which fires plastic bullets] and he instinctively swung it round and fired to save himself. He missed the guy's head by millimetres, and he was only about two feet from him. Larry hadn't even looked where he was shooting. It was pure survival instinct. Anyway, we had to let your man go. It was just too dangerous to carry on the arrest. The crowd was becoming increasingly confident, watching what had happened. It was now five-hundred-strong. They smelt blood. It's a very eerie, surreal situation, standing there exposed. They were throwing everything they could find at us, including petrol bombs. It seemed like there was millions of the bastards. You were also very conscious that if they managed to get you, they would kick you to death.

Both Larry and I tried to get into the front of the Land Rover. But with all the riot gear and the bulletproof vests we had on, we just wouldn't fit. I had no option but to try and get back in through the double doors I'd come out of at the back of the vehicle. Jim, a full-time reserve man, who had never been in a riot before, was holding the back doors

161

open and watching for me. I just had to go for it and hope for the best. I took a deep breath and fired a plastic bullet at the crowd, quite indiscriminately, I have to admit, and drew my revolver. The firing of the plastic bullet seemed to make them pause momentarily, just giving me enough time to get to the doors and throw myself in. I shouted, 'Go!' and we started to move off. Relief was flowing out of every pore in my body, as I started to take in my surroundings again. Jim had managed to shut the back doors, but was now sitting slumped forward with his head in his hands. The noise from the stones hitting the vehicle was unbelievable. I put my hands on Jim's shoulders, and pushed him back to try and get a look at him in the darkness. His face was just a mass of thick blood. He was drifting in and out of consciousness. I shouted to the driver to go straight to the hospital.

The rioters had pulled a plank with nails through it across the road in front of the Land Rover. We now had four flat tyres. The crowd started to rock the vehicle back and forth to topple it. We had no option but to try and get ourselves out of there and bring Jim to hospital. We drove through the rioters with the wheels completely flat. We had radioed for help, and two other vehicles came to our aid and escorted us. The Land Rover was driving on its wheel rims when we stopped. The smell of burning rubber was awful. The first priority was to get Jim help. No ambulance was going to get through to us, so Jim was put into one of the other vehicles and taken to hospital. The army arrived to give cover to our stranded Land Rover, in case of sniper attack or more rioters. I joined another crew and went back to the riot until my own crew got a new vehicle.

Jim was in hospital for a few weeks. His nose and jaw were badly broken, and he lost seven teeth. He'd opened the door for me with his visor up, and got hit full in the face with a half-brick. I don't think he's opened a door for me since.

Larry told me he had nightmares about firing the plastic bullet. It was luck and nothing else that he didn't kill that guy. He said he saw it in slow motion going past his head. It shows how easily these things happen. It was pure instinct to survive. Then when you got home after fourteen hours' duty, the wife would say, 'What a day I've had.' You just smiled to yourself and sympathised. Incidentally, we lifted the original skull [police jargon for a person] two days later.

01:16 – Crime Squad Office, Castlereagh Police Station, East Belfast

I was involved in the investigation into the murders of Corporals Howes and Wood, the two men who were pulled from a car and shot dead at an IRA funeral. The media held the key to all the events by way of witness accounts, the attack on the car and the photographic and video evidence they had. They are always very quick to point out where the police may stumble, but they weren't too quick to step up to the mark when they were the witnesses. Tracking and finding all the journalists was a major job. Finding and obtaining photographs, and the video evidence, was relatively straightforward in the UK, because legally they had to provide material. They didn't have to make witness statements but several of them did. We had so many media witnesses we were seeking, we ran out of alphabet to refer to them. It ended up there was a Witness A, and so on, and then Witness A1, B1, C1, because there were so many involved, including cameramen, soundmen, technicians, journalists, journalists' assistants.

The incident took place after the SAS intercepted three terrorists in Gibraltar, who were planning to blow up a band parade, and eliminated the threat. At the subsequent funeral of these IRA members, Michael Stone shot and killed three people, of whom one was reportedly an IRA man. Hence the reason the media were at the next funeral in such force. We even had to make an enquiry to Paris, because Channel 5 in Paris had some amazing footage of the attack.

At the scene, the IRA had seized tapes from camera crews and photographers. This particular cameraman had been intimidated at the scene and told to clear off. But he took up a position further up the road where he was able to pan in on this taxi. That turned out to be the taxi into which the two corporals were placed, en route to their execution across the road in Penny Lane. They were able to get a very good photographic image of a guy called Henry Maguire, who was in the front passenger seat. He shot his arm out in triumph and gave a triumphant salute to the onlookers. This was a very important piece of footage. I went to Paris and spoke to the cameraman. He said I could ask his news station for the tape. We went along to the offices of Channel 5 Television in Paris. We were shown into a nice room and were shown the footage we needed. then they said, 'Now you've seen it, you can't have it.' No amount of persuasion would change their mind. They didn't want to get involved as a media outlet to compromise their role.

We sat with the French detectives and mulled over what we should do late at night in our hotel room. The conversation developed somewhat, depending on drink. One of them had a girlfriend who worked at the news station, and he said, 'What if my friend was to produce a copy of this on the condition of anonymity?' I was then to go to court in Belfast and prove it came from an employee. But I wouldn't give her name. A tape was duly handed over by the detective, who said in all honesty that, 'Yes, this was prepared and made by an employee of the television company.' The tape was duly copied there, the original copy was put into a diplomatic bag and it came back via diplomatic channels to the Northern Ireland Office.

We made arrests based on footage from the copy. The images that were revealed from it helped to secure the conviction of one of the killers, who I think got around thirty years. He was wearing a white linen jacket and his face was instantly recognisable. Effectively the judge in the trial became a witness himself, because he could see what was presented in front of him.

01:20 – CID Office, Antrim Road Police Station, North Belfast

Some criminals are just inherently stupid. I was on night duty in the CID and I went for a bit of a drive round the area. Listening to the radio reports, I heard there had been a report of a robbery from a filling station. This guy had gone in and had run off with a bag of coal over his shoulder. Not the easiest thing to make your getaway on foot with. I was driving about, and I saw this guy down a side street with a bag of coal over his shoulder. He knew the police were after him, and he was fairly shifty. But I was in an unmarked CID car. I pulled up beside him and shouted, 'Get in.' He opened the back door, threw the bag of coal in and said, 'Thanks, mate.' Then I put the child locks on and drove him to Antrim Road Police Station. His face was a picture when he realised what he'd done. But we had a good laugh about it afterwards.

01:22 – Special Branch Office, Newry

The problem with the loyalist groups was that they would very often just get pissed and just decide right, let's go and kill a Catholic or a Shinner. There was no way of stopping it, because there was insufficient time. By comparison the

IRA tended to plan things days, weeks, even months in advance. This very often gave us a chance to intercept it. The INLA [Irish National Liberation Army] were like the Prods. They would also just get pissed up and say, 'Let's go and shoot somebody.'

Very few informants work for you full time. People talk about collusion, thinking agents are under control. Actually the agent is only ever under control when he's actually talking to you face-to-face. The rest of the time they can do whatever the hell they want and frequently do. Sometimes IRA men who were agents would tell their handlers nothing was happening. Then in the next day or two, those same agents were out shooting at the army or the police, and they were shot dead.

In my entire career, I never heard of them ever getting a 'get out of jail free' card, apart from those dealt out by the government and senior civil servants in the NIO. I can only think of a few that I ever had anything to do with that were totally trustworthy. The remainder you could not have trusted them at all. Coming up to Christmas, they were all making up stuff because they needed a wee bonus for the holidays. They either gave us something deliberately to get money or they just made something up. We would be running around in circles come Christmas, because the rest of the year the information was good. So you couldn't take a chance.

It's a very important point – the one about the degree of control you had over informants. It was minimal. There were also so many people out there who worked for us for a year or two and then got cold feet and then pulled back. Attempts would be made to recruit them again – sometimes they were successful and sometimes they weren't. But there were a large number who worked for us at some time or another. I would put it at about 80 to 85 per cent of republican terrorists – not all career informants, but people who spoke to us at some point. Thankfully – as some people have worked out – some very senior members of the Provisional IRA and Sinn Féin were among them. They didn't tell you everything about themselves, although they told you plenty about everyone else.

01:33 – CID Office, New Barnsley Police Station, West Belfast

The divisional commander held a briefing where he told CID that a Protestant had been kidnapped, and was being held somewhere in west Belfast. It was a race to try and find this person alive. We were even out in our own cars doing patrols in plainclothes, looking for anything out of place. A very dangerous practice for a police officer in west Belfast.

We got told to abandon the search and sent to a call at Ton Street. The call was an arson at a house, with one fatality reported. I went into the house. I saw this person sitting on the chair. The odd thing that stayed with me was the expression on his face. He looked really frightened. He was burnt to a cinder. The report of the incident had come from the victim's wife. She suspected her son, Anthony Shields, had committed the murder of his father. I decided to wait until after the funeral, then I arrested the son. He was only thirteen. I lay in bed the night before. I didn't know what my first question was going to be. I couldn't stop thinking about the interview, with him being so young. When I brought him in, my first question was very simple: 'Anthony, why did you kill your father?' I near fell out of the chair when he replied, 'Because he wouldn't give me my pocket money.'

His father had come in very drunk. Anthony had asked for his pocket money but he refused. When the father fell asleep, the young fella packed papers all round him, even into his pockets. He then set fire to the papers and went outside to watch. The fire took hold very quickly. I charged him with murder and he was sent to Lisnevin young offenders centre on the outskirts of Belfast. He had admitted everything, accurately fitting the evidence.

About two or three years later, I was in bed. I got a phone call from Paddy Hunt, a detective inspector. 'Harry, that young fella you charged with the murder of his father, where is he at the minute?' I said he was in Lisnevin. Paddy said, 'I'm very busy, would you do me a favour and ring and make sure he's still there?' I rang Lisnevin. It was about three o'clock in the morning, and I asked the fella who answered the phone if he was still in custody. He said he was. I said to him, 'I know this sounds a bit strange, but would you mind going to his cell and checking?' It took him about fifteen minutes to come back. He said, 'Yes, he's fast asleep.' I rang Paddy back and asked him what was the interest. He said, 'We found his mother a couple of hours ago, burnt to a cinder at her house in the exact same way as the father.'

The strange thing is when we got the report from the pathologist after the young fella admitted the father's murder, I went to see the pathologist. I asked if he could tell me if there was any carbon monoxide in the father's lungs. He made a few enquiries, rang me back and said, 'We'll have to get this body exhumed, there was no carbon monoxide in the lungs.' Then about an hour later he rang me back, and he told me forensic had made a mistake. There was a very slight trace in the lungs. If the father had no carbon monoxide in his lungs, he was dead when the fire started. They never found out who killed the mother. Now, despite the son's confession, we don't really know what happened to either of them. I also suspect the father's lungs were clear. Now there's a mystery.

01:46 – Crime Squad, South Region

Stress is something we all know about now. But the concept was unheard of in the police in the 1970s and 1980s. I know a Christian policeman and I used to marvel that he could he could deal with all the shit we were investigating. But he had his faith, he believed in the afterlife. Ben Ford, you called him. Ben worked with me when I was in the crime squad. Ben's approach was always one of salvation and that worked for him.

Mostly the rest of us dealt with it with alcohol. I had joined the police in 1972, and I didn't drink or smoke until 1980, when I went into the flying squad. I was with forty other men, travelling all over Northern Ireland, interviewing terrorists all the time, assisting the local CID in murders, bombings and shootings. When you finished your interviews, you went back to the hotel and if you didn't drink, you weren't fully part of the team. To help you cope with work, your medication was your drink. We took a brave bit of medication.

02:05 – Coffee Break

There are a lot of sad memories, too, boys committing suicide. I don't know what excuses they made, or what excuse can you make. I have always considered it as a cowardly way out. There were so many people who were so messed up from some of the incidents. It was so sad when you heard. You'd think, 'Why did you not come and talk to me?'

There was a big mate, Joe, he's supposed to have killed himself in Ards, one of the best guys I knew. His whole family is in the police. We were in the DMSU together, did all the Grand Prixs and stuff together, great guy and lovely family. I know his brothers and sister and his mum. He just couldn't take it. His girlfriend, he loved her. She was seeing somebody else. They were off and on, and I had said to him, 'It's looks like she's going out with this other guy.' He went round one night. But the other guy was there. He was another peeler, and he turns round and calls her upstairs. She said he tried to do the two of them. He committed suicide. He shot himself. It tortures me. We could have tried to sort it out. You just feel helpless, and there are so many, so many like that. Whether it's a cry for help or what, people have tried it.

So many marriages ended as well. It's not because of the drinking. It's because of the Troubles. The pressure takes on a life of its own, and people don't even realise it's building up in them. The problem is we had a gun, whereas a normal person would have had to think, 'How I am going to do this?' and plan it. Then the next day, they would have sobered up. Cops had the solution beside them in the form of a .357 Magnum gun. It was all too easy to end it in a second.

02:07 – CID Office, Tennent Street Police Station, North Belfast

A guy had his house burgled in the north of the city. He was a young red-headed guy, who was in his final year of university. This particular break-in happened just as he was studying for his finals. The usual stuff had been taken: TV, video recorder, anything that could be sold quickly for a few quid. The only thing he wanted back was his briefcase, which contained a lot of his course notes from college. They had taken him years, quite literally, to write up. The notes were critical to him trying to revise for his finals. He was obviously very upset about losing them and panicking about studying for his exams without them. After a couple of days, we did get his notes back. The thieves had realised the notes were no use to them, and dumped them and the briefcase on some wasteground. A couple of kids found the bag and got in touch with the police. I recognised from the description he had given me that it was your man's study notes. I was really delighted for him and took great pleasure in bringing the case back to him at the house. When he saw what I had for him, he was quite emotional. He thought they were gone forever. He just couldn't stop thanking me. We had a bit of a laugh about how things sometimes turn out all right. I wished him the best of luck with his exams and we shook hands, with him promising to let me know how he got on. Nice lad.

About a week or so later, the wee lad was out walking close to where he lived. It was about two o'clock in the morning. He was just getting his head cleared after a long night's studying. He was walking along the footpath, heading back to the house, when one of those murder gangs came up and shot him in the back of the head. It was just before he was to sit his finals. It was a pure sectarian murder, just that terrible part of living where he did. A young man trying to better himself, with his whole life ahead of him, slaughtered in the street. When I think of the poor lad just days before, worried so much about his exams, and his pure delight at getting his study notes back – he never even got doing his exams.

02:09 – Eglinton Barracks, Londonderry

There was a military married quarters in Eglinton for the regiments who were stationed there two years. You got to know people over time, including the army, because you were out working with them. I got quite friendly with this family from the barracks. They were lovely people. They had a baby that they absolutely adored. Then tragedy struck. I had to deal with it. We got a call to a sudden death, which police attend to rule out foul play. This was the death of a baby of about ten weeks. The child died in the cot, but it wasn't a cot death. The cot had been supplied by the army.

The mattress supplied by the army was smaller than the cot and the child slipped down in between the mattress and the wooden bars of the cot, and suffocated. I had to attend the post-mortem, as well as deal with the family. You could not imagine anything worse. There were pressure marks on the child's back from the bars of the cot pressing against it when the child became wedged. For the post-mortem, they had to take the cot and mattress from the house, and the pathologist worked, pulled and turned with the dead child, until he matched everything up to satisfy himself it was an accident. Because I knew the people, it made it really difficult to deal with. God help them, even trying to get over that. That affected me for a long time. Many things affected me in the police over the years, especially anything that involved children. Just tragic.

02:19 – Donegall Pass Police Station, South Belfast

Quite often the Samaritans would be phoned to say there was a bomb at such and such a location, and you've got twenty minutes to get them out, or something of that ilk. This night, we got a report that a phone call was made to a radio station to say there was a bomb at the Samaritans' offices, which were at the bottom of the Lisburn Road. We were convinced it was a mistake. We were thinking, 'The Samaritans have been phoned about a bomb, but there won't be a bomb actually in the Samaritans!'

Anyway, we went round to see if we could get to the bottom of it. There was an elderly man working in the Samaritans building that night. It was after eleven o'clock at night. I said, 'Anything strange happening today? Anybody different been in? Workmen or anybody odd, or that could have maybe left something somewhere?' You were worried about firebombs and things at that time. The guy said, 'No, no. There's been nothing like that. There's been absolutely nobody in here. Sure, who's going to want to blow this place up?' I was pretty much agreeing with him!

We had a good search around the place, couldn't see anything. But just as we got to the bottom of the stairs, I looked in behind the door. There was this small airline bag that people would wear over their shoulder when they were travelling. I lifted it up and looked into it. There was a towel on top, and underneath was this box of putty-looking stuff, with a motorcycle battery attached to a clock, which I could hear ticking. The three of us – myself, the policeman I was with, and the old boy – ran straight out the door.

Opposite their building was the Russell Court Hotel, with the road up the side of it. We took off like Olympic sprinters. I think the old man was going faster than anyone. Halfway across the road, I realised I was still holding the bloody bomb. I just ended up throwing it backwards over my shoulder towards the building we had just come out of. We called out the army technical officer, and they duly arrived. They managed to get the thing defused. But I always look back on that, you know, taking the flipping bomb with me. It wasn't the brightest thing to do.

02:37 – Andersonstown Police Station, West Belfast

I was in Andersonstown police station. The IRA had abandoned a lorry across the gates to the station, with a suspect device in it. It was trapping all personnel within the station, although there was another way out. It was a hidden exit only to be used in emergencies. There were quite a number of people in the yard, trying to make decisions about what they were going to do, when gunfire erupted. It was being fired into the yard. Bullets were landing all around the blast walls of the station, and indeed on the carpark and the yard. Plenty of policemen were about, and they all returned fire. A gun battle broke out. It must have raged for about forty minutes. It then started to rain a bit. You could see the policemen looking at each other. There's an old adage that a good policeman doesn't get wet. The rain started to get heavier and heavier. Without anyone saying anything, they started to get into the back of armoured Land Rovers, which were bulletproof. Then the IRA went away as well. During a very ferocious battle in the middle of the city, rain stopped play, as if it was Lord's and the umpire pulled stumps. Fortunately there was no one hurt on the police side. I don't know about the other side.

02:39 – Londonderry

My first day's duty was on Bloody Sunday. I was due to start work at Tennent Street on Monday but I was called in early because a young police officer had been shot dead and a lot of the lads in the station wanted to go to the funeral.

So, they called me at home and I started on the Sunday. I was transported to Londonderry and put on the junction of William Street and John Street, the coldest place on earth. I stood there all day. I didn't hear any shooting. But sometime during the shift, we could hear some kind of confrontation between the army and the crowd. There were reports of injuries. A bit further along the road from my particular point, a car was stopped and there was a dead body in it. Apparently this guy was being transported to hospital. It was too late for him. He was stopped by the army and I was told there was a blast bomb in his pocket.

02:40 – On Patrol, South Belfast

Ulster's finest [an ironic reference to loyalist paramilitaries] had decided to go down to plant a bomb at a bar called the Jubilee, just off the Ormeau Road. They were driving a Morris 1100, and had brought the bomb in a gas cylinder.

They had a Sterling submachine gun in case something went wrong. The gun was brand new. They had made the gun themselves, but had managed somehow to get the working parts for the firing mechanism from the factory. They were reject parts, but they had some source was able to get them for 'the cause'.

They got the bomb's fuse lit. The guy got out, ran over and threw it into the hallway in the pub. He turned round and jumped back into the car to escape. An older man was coming out of the pub quite drunk. When the gas cylinder landed on him, he picked it up and threw it back at the car. It went into the back seat and landed beside the bomber who had just left it.

When the bomber threw it into the pub, it had landed on its end and had actually put the fuse out. So it wasn't going to blow up anyway. But they took off through the side streets in a panic, turned a corner and drove into an army Saracen [personnel carrier]. Those things weigh tonnes, but in the excitement the car didn't realise. The Saracen wouldn't have even noticed, anyway. To add to their woes, the army had an observation post in the gasworks. They saw the guy get out with the Sterling. One of their people shot him dead in the back of the car. The car drove off again. They then made it through the side streets and up as far as University Street. They turned a corner and drove into an RUC Land Rover. They couldn't quite understand what was going on. They were having these accidents, and nothing was happening about it.

They ended up parking up – I suppose to see what was going on. But they didn't know what to do. The patrol I was in came along, but drove past. We saw the two guys sitting in the car, but we didn't really think that much about them. Someone had also just been shot dead at the bottom of the Ormeau Road. We thought that perhaps they were just waiting on someone. It was a perfectly normal thing for them to be doing. If they were the gunmen, they would have driven off!

About an hour later, we were back in that area and they were still sitting there. Eventually we got out and went over to speak to them. We found one guy was sitting there dead. The other one was sitting with a bomb between his knees. One cop said, 'What's with the gas cylinder?' The guy said, 'It's a bomb.' I think they didn't know what to do. So they just sat there, waiting to be arrested. I mean honestly, I think there's days you could be forgiven for thinking the Prods just weren't cut out for this.

03:47 – Uniform Patrol, North Belfast

Some people had seen some guys breaking into a school in north Belfast. A school is a big area to try and go through. This was literally during the night, so there was no one there to help. We were able to get into it okay, but the place was so vast to try and catch a couple of people on the premises. We decided to send for the dog section men, who were on duty that night. They arrived. Of course the old dog's lying sleeping in the back of the truck. The handler went round to him. The dog looks up, and then the handler starts patting him, and half-thumping him in a friendly way around the head. He said, 'Where's the bad boys? Where's the bad boys?' The old dog went from half-asleep to having the ears pricked up. The dog jumped up and down, ready to play cops and robbers.

All we had to do was open the door that the burglars had forced entry through and just let the dogs in. The dogs were let off their leads and with a final shout of, 'Get the bad boys,' off they went in search of their quarry. We then took a walk through the place after them. We found these two fellows standing with their backs totally pressed into the wall, scared to move. The dog was sitting in front of them. If they blinked, the dog went grrrrrrrrr. They were very glad to see us to get away from the dogs. It was the funniest thing. These two tough boys breaking in there and being rounded up like sheep. The work those dogs do is unbelievable. They do the work of forty men in those circumstances.

03:48 – Roslea Police Station, County Fermanagh

Some things you can't explain. Maybe some things are best left unexplained. This is going back to Roslea Station in Fermanagh. A number of us were living in the station. About four o'clock one morning, there was an almighty explosion. Everybody woke up, wondering what it was. The whole area was immediately placed out of bounds to all patrols in case of secondary devices. In the morning light, they got an army helicopter to fly over the area to see what had happened. They could see the road had been blown apart as the result of a massive landmine explosion. We didn't know if it was an own goal they'd scored [terrorists blown themselves up planting the device], or what.

There was a policeman stationed near us who didn't drive. Every Monday, he got the bus down to Fivemiletown, and the police went up and collected him. When Special Branch got the intelligence in, it transpired the bomb was designed for the police car that afternoon going to pick him up. When the ATO [bomb disposal] came in and examined the scene, there was no sign of any bodies around. This was strange because if this thing had gone off prematurely when it was being planted, there should have been. It had obviously had been set properly with a view to murdering police. It remained a bit of a mystery.

About a month later, I was out with the army on a foot patrol across the fields where that explosion had occurred.

A local boy lived there with this brother, a farmer. He invited us in for a cup of tea. As is always the case, the locals know everything. The police are usually the last to know. The oul' boy said to me, 'That woman was very lucky three or four weeks ago.' I didn't want to appear stupid, so I said something vague like, 'She was lucky, all right.' I didn't want to show my hand that I didn't know what he was talking about. He said, 'If she'd been there a couple of seconds earlier, that car of hers would have been blown off the road.' Apparently this woman had been up visiting people in the area and was on her way back home at the time these boys had been setting up the ambush. It was the dead of night. She was driving a Mark IV Cortina, a very common vehicle in general police use. Rather than take the chance, the bombers thought, 'We'll just detonate it and leave.' A very lucky escape for all.

03:49 – Twinbrook Estate, West Belfast

In Twinbrook, up in west Belfast, this day, it was just wild. It was like cowboys and Indians. There were pockets of disorder everywhere. Petrol bombs, bricks, nuts and bolts were being thrown at us. Anything they could get their hands on. The reporters were starting it. No sooner would a camera crew arrive in the area, and you would have a riot on your hands. To be fair, foreign crews were the worst. They would pay to get good shots of petrol bombers – sometimes having several takes. So you were shooting plastic bullets at the petrol bomber beside the reporter. And if you were unfortunate enough to miss the petrol bomber, well, so be it!

03:52 – Hastings Street Police Station, West Belfast

We were coming back to the base at Hastings Street. A high-velocity shot was fired at us. It was clearly a sniper, and we all had the impression it was coming from Divis Flats. A quick-thinking soldier that was with us stopped a lorry, crawled underneath and used the lorry as cover. The chief inspector came out to see what was happening. He couldn't believe a shot had been fired. He started asking things like, 'Was there a car backfired?' You would like to think he would have known enough to tell the difference between a shooting and a car. Anyway, when we got in to the station I got changed and was about to go home. I had finished my shift for the day. The chief said, 'Where are you going, sergeant? I want you to take a patrol back out straight away.' One of the other lads from the unit said, 'Why, do you want to give the sniper a second chance?' I can tell you by the time that we went back out on patrol, the gunman was probably on his third pint of Guinness in the local republican club.

04:22 – Special Branch Office, County Armagh

I certainly came across instances of collusion in which the IRA had recruited people in various organisations – for example, from within British Telecom because they could get an ex-directory number identified faster than we could. They recruited one guy who was a telephone engineer but he eventually left BT and had to go on the run down south because he was discovered to have been making the circuit boards for the bombs, including the timer power units.

One policeman I know had to move home on several occasions. They could never figure out how it was the IRA always got on to him so quickly. It turned out the IRA had somebody in an insurance brokerage, and the one thing the boy did was re-insure his car every year through the same brokerage. So every time he moved to a new house, the IRA had his new address and went around and tried to kill him.

There was a big drive to get more Catholics in the civil service and there were numerous sympathisers who slipped through the net, some of them at a reasonably elevated level, which was quite disturbing. And they had the Brew [dole] offices, hospital records – they had their sources who would supply the records – taxi drivers, the DVLA and the banks. I won't even begin about the legal profession. It was very loaded. So there was a huge amount of collusion went on.

Remember the young paratrooper who was shot dead down at The Arches in east Belfast? It was just at the end of the campaign. He had been stationed at Palace Barracks in Holywood. He flew back to see his girlfriend here, got into a taxi at the airport and got taken straight to the front door of her house. With the English accent, the taxi driver started chatting to find out what he could about him. The taxi dropped him off, he went straight in and saw his girlfriend while the taxi driver watched. The following night, the IRA came round and shot him dead.

05:00 – Carrickmore Police Station, County Tyrone

In the mid-1980s I was the station sergeant at Carrickmore RUC Station. A foot patrol had been out in the early hours of the morning, and they had stopped a woman in a car. We knew who she was and that she didn't work, nor did she smoke. She was actually in charge of Cumann na mBan – the women's division of the IRA – in Mid Ulster. They stopped her, searched her and questioned her in relation to what she was doing there. They found numerous bits and pieces of interest along with various documents in her vehicle. I'll just read out here from the report, verbatim: 'In her car they seized a packet of sandwiches, a flask, an address book, a packet of twenty cigarettes, one lighter, one camera and, last but not least, a tub of Flora margarine.' These items were seized under emergency legislation. The address book could have been suspicious enough, as could the camera.

Bearing in mind that she didn't smoke or work and because of the flask and sandwiches, the boys thought maybe she was heading away to a couple of fellow terrorists lying out up the hills. Maybe they were waiting to detonate a bomb when a security force patrol was passing.

So they seized this stuff. They arrived back into the station with it. They told me what had happened. I told them to record what they seized in the special property register. I said, 'Photocopy the stuff out of the book, take the film out of the camera in case there's anything worth looking at.' Really what you should have done is hold it for a day or two, and then given it back. They said, 'How long will we hold it for?' I said, 'The only problem I can see here are the sandwiches.' Because obviously they were perishable.

The next day, the peeler doing communications was upstairs. I heard the phone ringing, as it was above my office. He buzzed down and said, 'Danny Morrison [Sinn Féin MP for Mid Ulster at that time] is on the phone. He wants to speak to the station sergeant.' I was stuck, as the inspector was off, so I said, 'Put him through.' I knew rightly the boys in the station were listening, because you could hear the echo on the line. He said, 'I'll tell you what it is, sergeant. One of my constituents ...' I knew exactly what was coming and I knew what the problem was going to be. He carried on: 'One of my constituents was stopped yesterday morning. Are you aware of the incident?' I said, 'I am.' He said, 'The problem is she had several items seized under emergency legislation. Can you tell me exactly what is going to happen to these items?' I said, 'They'll be returned in due course.'

Then the sixty-four million dollar question was: 'What about the sandwiches, because obviously they're perishable?' And it's quoted here in the complaint he made against me for my attitude: 'When challenged the next day for the return of the items, including the sandwiches as they are perishable, RUC Sergeant C. XXX mirthfully declared, "Sure if they are hard she can always toast them."'

06:04 – Springfield Road Police Station, West Belfast

The camaraderie that built up along the way was fantastic and something I miss most. The tighter the station, the better it was. That friendship for most people just stays forever. We had a great team down in Newry. We actually had a Thursday morning club and a Thursday night club, when we finished night shift on Thursday morning. Depending where you lived, half would go to somebody's house, say in Banbridge, and would drink into the afternoon, and then sleep it off or get taxis home. The rest of them would go down to the Windsor in Bangor on the Thursday night. I actually made both once. I slept for two days after it!

06:05 – Crime Squad, Castlereagh Police Station, East Belfast

We had information that the Ulster Defence Association had been taking a crowd of young lads up into the hills around Belfast to train them up on using various weapons. We decided to arrest a pile of them. So we organised a big lift. The UDA were carrying out exercises to get their field badges. I was in the crime squad when they were all arrested. One boy we scooped had left during the exercise early because he had tins of beans with him and he had no tin opener. My job was to interview this other idiot. It was the same old story – we used to say, 'It has to be a Prod job if it goes pear-shaped.' These boys were preparing for a 'doomsday situation' with the IRA. You couldn't make it up, very serious stuff.

This peeler with me interviewing was called Jackie

Thompson. Jackie's got a bad stutter sometimes. He was trying to talk to the prisoner, and when the boy starting talking back to him, it turned out he had a stutter as well. He had never been in a police station before, so that was making him stutter all the more, because he was nervous. I think Jackie was going to hit him a slap because he thought he was taking the piss. Eventually he asked him, 'What was your role in this military exercise up the hills?' He said, 'C-c-c-c-c-c-communications.' He was the radio operator. We burst out laughing.

06:07 – Woodburn Police Station, West Belfast

During the hunger strikes, we were sitting around Suffolk whenever Bobby Sands died. All hell broke loose. People were out on the streets protesting, banging all the bin lids they could get on the road. We were just there to make sure there wasn't going to be an attack on the Orange area of Suffolk from the Catholic side. There must have been fifteen vehicles down the road. We were there at the shops, keeping an eye on what was going on. The whistles were going, the loud hailer and the bin lids. That horrible sound of bin lids on the ground.

The next minute, one of the Land Rovers further up got whacked. They opened up with automatic fire on it. We were just sitting, assessing the situation in the relative safety of the vehicle, which was bulletproof. Nothing was happening. Then the crowd started coming towards us, hundreds of them.

New Barnsley Station was under attack. New Barnsley had gone through thousands of baton rounds that night. They actually ran out of baton rounds at one stage. We said we didn't need as many as fifteen vehicles here. Everybody was busting to get doing something. They all wanted to get at it to help their mates. The crowd attacking New

Barnsley was huge and the order was given for the cops inside to draw rifles. It was the only option left. Then the army appeared and broke through to the station. I wouldn't like to guess how many people would have been killed if the army hadn't turned up.

There was another guy I worked with, Peter G. If you went to his house, he'd say, 'That's the Patsy O'Hara driveway,' and 'That's the Bobby Sands bathroom suite.' He'd named all the new things he'd bought from all the overtime after the hunger strikers!

06:09 – CID Office, Omagh Police Station, County Tyrone

I had to move home several times under threat. Moving home is a stressful thing at the best of times. But in those circumstances it is very disturbing and disruptive for the family. I have two sons, one who was practically minded and very skilled with his hands. A good career as a craftsman beckoned. The other lad, he was very academically minded. He got his 11-plus, went to grammar school and was doing very well in class. His results were excellent and the teachers all felt he would go to university with a bright future to look forward to.

I had to move home under threat on three occasions in three years. That meant he went to three different grammar schools in different towns in that time. It affected him psychologically more than we realised. Each grammar school, there seemed to be a different curriculum or a different way to tackle the syllabus. New teachers to get used to as well. Every time he was getting to grips with the change he was moved again, having to make new friends. Plus knowing that my life was under threat didn't help.

When it came time to do his GCSE exams at sixteen, he just broke down under the pressure. There was no doubt he had the ability, if he had been left alone. If he could have stayed at the first grammar school or perhaps even the second. But the third one was just too much for him. He stuck at it as best he could. He really was very intelligent. But when it came to the pressure of trying to catch up and to do well in the circumstances, he just broke. I like to think of him as a survivor because he has come through it. But you could interpret that his whole life was perhaps destroyed by what happened. He could have done well, perhaps have gone to university, who knows. I just feel it was my fault. Don't get me wrong, the police were very good to me in many ways. But when I think about the impact it had on the kids. He is now still sitting to this day with virtually no qualifications and just getting what work he can. I put this down to me, and I know I shouldn't. I feel so guilty about it. I blame myself because if I had been in a different job ... I beat myself at times over the head because of that. I still do even now.

06:30 – Major Investigation Team (MIT) Office, North Queen Street Police Station, Belfast City Centre

One of the cases I dealt with was a young guy called David Cupples. David lived in Dundonald. He worked in the kitchens in an army barracks near the Crumlin Road. His father used to drop him over, and sometimes he even walked from Dundonald. Because of the threat from the IRA to anyone entering or leaving at the back gate of the camp, he didn't want his father to drop him at the gate. This was in case his car registration number was picked up by IRA spotters. That would have allowed them to maybe follow him home to line him up to be murdered, or even just to spot the car in traffic to kill him there. So he used to drop him down at the Mater Hospital. Then David would walk up the Crumlin Road and turn right into Clifton Park Avenue and down in through the backs of the houses to the barracks. On this particular morning at about 6.30 a.m, David was dropped off by his dad near the hospital and walked up to approach the army base on foot. At the same time, William Hill, one of Johnny Adair's henchmen, was coming out of the loyalist estate across the road from the hospital in the Lower Shankill. He had been drinking in one of the loyalist dens, had fallen out with his girlfriend and stormed off from the party. Hill was heading towards home when he saw David Cupples, and decided he was probably a Catholic, because he was walking on the wrong side of the road.

He was walking on the right-hand side of the Crumlin Road up towards Clifton Park Avenue, which would have taken you beyond Summer Street, which was the Prods' side. So, if you were looking at him, you would probably have thought he was a Catholic because of the area he was walking towards. It really was that easy to get yourself murdered in Belfast.

A woman who looked out her window saw David lying by the roadside, trying to get up. He kept falling back. She heard him calling out for his mother. The woman had a phone in the house and she rang the police. The ambulance arrived at the scene first and initially they thought that he had been knocked down. She didn't see the incident happen. They thought he could be treated at the scene, but then they realised he had serious head injuries. His mother had died just three years earlier of cancer. I don't even know why that sticks in my head. He was still alive but braindead effectively. Ironically, he was taken to the Mater Hospital. They decided there was no hope for him and turned off the machine.

I dealt a lot with his father, John Cupples who was a lovely man, a really lovely guy. We worked hard with him and we really did a good investigation. This guy who was wanted for the murder was on the run for about a month.

We searched high and low on the Shankill to try and flush him out. We thought if we tortured the locals hard enough, they would hand him over. He wouldn't have been the first paramilitary to be told by his bosses to go and hand himself in to take the heat off them. But we just couldn't get him. We searched anything and everything. Eventually it worked and he ended up handing himself into Tennent Street Police Station on New Year's Day, when he knew the police would be at low strength.

We discovered there was a video. Afterwards, he topped up his phone in the garage at the corner of Clifton Park Avenue, where he was caught on video. He must have been thinking about everything and he went back to the garage the next day to try and get the video. Thankfully the staff had the wisdom to say, 'The video's not here,' but it actually was there. But on its own, it didn't prove anything. We still had to prove that he did the murder. But it put him at the scene near the time of the murder, which was a start. We then went into a massive investigation as now we had a suspect. I think it's the only time in my life that someone has pleaded guilty to murder on circumstantial evidence. That would normally be a definite fight in court. When he eventually pleaded guilty, he got fourteen years jail, which was diabolical in my view. He had sat during interview making paper darts and throwing them at the detectives. Even his own solicitor gave up on him, saying to us when he came out of the interview room, 'I don't know how you boys stick this.'

John Cupples wrote a cheque at the end of it all to the Police Benevolent Fund as an expression of his gratitude for the effort put in by detectives to catch his son's murderer. During the investigation, we intercepted the killer's mail. He was writing to his girlfriend. This actually put an end to him. She got frightened because she had fallen out with him. She was from a really good family and he was writing to her threatening all sorts of things. It was to be the final nail in his coffin, because he didn't know we were intercepting his mail. When it was intercepted, we were photocopying to a very high standard and the photocopy was going back into the envelope and going to the girlfriend's house. We were reading all his mail and in it he admitted bombing the political office of the SDLP on the Antrim Road. He was convicted of that as well.

We then went with a search warrant to the girlfriend's house and recovered all the copied letters. We had kept the original letters to use as evidence. Those were the sort of things we were doing. You had to think wisely with these guys, thinking outside the box. It was all done legally. No one had told us to do it, but we did and we got him.

When he'd gone to do the bombing at the SDLP offices, he'd worn a Celtic football top, because the office was on the Antrim Road around the Waterworks, which is a nationalist area. That was the Prods' disguise in the Catholic areas.

06:57 – Uniform Patrol, County Fermanagh

There is nothing more dangerous than a bored policeman. Whenever 'Robert' [a nickname the police use to describe themselves] was out in the car and got bored, that was when he was at his most dangerous and mischievous. I was out in the local divisional mobile patrol car this day and it was really quiet. I don't think we'd had a call all day. So we were just travelling along through the countryside, trying to get the day in, when the observer, who was obviously bored, decided to break the tedium. He lifted the radio mike and said into it, 'I'm a cunt.' That was all he said, and that was transmitted right across the entire division. We waited, and waited, but nothing happened. After about five minutes, he lifted the mike again and said into it, 'I'm a cunt.' We waited and once again nothing. No response from anyone. He gives it ten minutes and once again transmits, 'I'm a cunt,' throughout the division. Finally, the divisional communications rooms in Enniskillen came on the radio and transmitted to all the cars in L division, 'Would the man calling himself that name please desist at once, and report to this communications centre immediately?' So the guy lifted the mike and said, 'I might be a cunt. But I'm not a stupid cunt!'

06:58 – CID Office, Musgrave Street Police Station, Belfast City Centre

One night an Argos store was burnt to the ground. This was the big Argos at the corner of Cornmarket, right bang in the city centre. This was right at the height of the Troubles, when the IRA were destroying a lot of property with either car or firebombs. The detective sergeant and I started investigating this big fire the next day, once the ground had cooled a bit. Between ourselves and speaking to the fire service, we pretty quickly found the seat of the fire. But something about it just didn't look right to us. No matter what explanation or possibility you came up with, it still didn't look right. Something was wrong, we just hadn't worked out what yet.

We established the fire had started round by the manager's office, so we went on with enquiries as to how it happened. We found out that the manager had been off that night and the alarm hadn't been working, which immediately got our alarm bells ringing. We dug a bit further into it and the person we went to speak to was the deputy manager. It turned out the deputy was a good golfer, who had also suddenly appeared at his golf club with a swanky new car. He also bought his mate's mother a brand-new fur coat. So I thought, 'Right, that's enough to give him a tug, bring him in for questioning. He must know something about it.'

I got him to admit that he knew that the safe had contained a lot of money. He also admitted he was aware the alarm system wasn't working that well. Once he had broken and started to talk, it was only a matter of time before he coughed up the rest of it.

Eventually he admitted that, on the evening of the fire, before he left the store, he had jammed the door of the fire escape, so it couldn't shut. Then he went up to meet his mate at Fortwilliam Golf Club, not that far from the city centre. They had a few drinks, no doubt making sure he was seen by everyone to build an alibi for later use. He then told his mate that he had just remembered something he had forgotten to do, but he would be back shortly. He shot back to the store and went in through the fire escape door, which he had left ajar. He of course knew where the safe was and where the manager kept the key. He opened the safe and took about £15,000 with him. That was a great deal of money then. He took the money, closed up but then as an afterthought he thought he would cover his backside a bit. He found some straw which was used for packaging goods sold in the store. He then lit it near the manager's office and up it went. The fire of course got out of control very quickly and by the time he was back in Fortwilliam, which would have been roughly about an hour since he had left the club, the whole building was ablaze. Why he lit it, I don't know. But he caused hundreds of thousands of pounds worth of damage even back then. Watching too much TV, I suppose.

I thought that was that, case closed. The next thing was we got a report of a burglary at the jewellery store next door to the now burnt-out Argos. Stranger still, it happened between the shop being locked for the night before the fire started and the time when the owners were allowed to return to the premises by the fire department and the police when it was safe to do so. Up until then it would have been preserved as a crime scene and closed off. It turned out the jewellery store had to have been broken into either as the fire was being put out, or in the immediate aftermath. We looked at it and thought about it from every possible angle. Lo and behold, it had to be the fire brigade, they were the only people with the access to all the buildings in the timeframe. So when they got in, they must have stolen the missing jewellery.

Because of the number of suspects involved I needed help. A temporary squad was put together to coordinate the arrests and searches so they all happened at the same time. Obviously this was done to stop them warning each other and destroying evidence. We hit every fire station in Belfast, searched all their lockers, as well as going to firemen's houses where we found jewellery buried in the garden, up in the roof spaces, all over the place. We got everything. They had all been caught sleeping. A number of firemen were prosecuted and jailed. The deputy manager of Argos went to prison as well. That case always stuck with me. I hate to see members of the emergency services letting themselves, their colleagues and their families down like that. Shame on them – they got what they deserved.

Once again I thought that was that. I can finally forget about the Argos incident; case closed. Until, it must have been about eighteen months later, I was sitting having my lunch in Musgrave Street Station and I got a call that there was a body round at High Street/Cornmarket. I went round and the workmen had been digging the foundations for a replacement building. Argos had been completely knocked down. As they dug down for the foundations, they came across a body. I reckoned it was about eight foot down below the ground level. I remember the bones were black and I called the bosses down to have a look. I also got the forensics team to call round.

It became obvious it wasn't a murder, or certainly not a recent one, as the remains were too far down into the ground. The bones too were very black. The forensics man, when he was down in the pit, handed me up a skull with a hole in the back of the head. And the bones had, like, wee shells on them. It was very strange. I was thinking about all the possible answers there could be as to how the body got there. I thought it was maybe someone that had been killed during the Blitz when Belfast was badly bombed during the Second World War. I was left to carry on the investigation. A lady from forensics, Judy I think you called her, she had taken the bones to be examined up in the forensics lab on the other side of Belfast. So she and I had a chat as to what age the bones could be. She came to the conclusion they were probably about three or four hundred years old. And no, I'm not going to tell you we had found the Irish hide and seek champion.

Forensics did further research on the skull. In the past, boats came up into Belfast as far as Arthur Street. They thought it could have been a sailor that had been washed ashore. The hole in the back of the head looked like a musket hole. They reckoned he would have been about twenty-five years of age because of the teeth.

Across the road from where the body was found used to be Belfast Prison. At the end of the street was the public hanging place. So we thought maybe it was a prisoner who had been hanged inside the prison. It's interesting to find out how many things in Belfast go back hundreds of years. So I was happy enough that we couldn't go any further with the case. It was just going to be guesswork.

The next thing to be sorted out was what to do with what, at the end of the day, were human remains. Do you give it a Christian burial or what? Do we go to a church? I remember going up to forensics and the skull had all been cleaned up. It was nice and white. It actually looked like it was just made of plastic. It was so clean, as were the teeth. That night, when I was making enquiries about what to do with the skull and the bones, they blew up the forensics laboratory, and the poor bugger was blown up with it. He didn't have much luck. I never did find out where he came from. To be left to rest in peace where he was for hundreds of years, and then the IRA blew him up.

06:59 – Uniform Patrol, West Belfast

When you went in to start the early turn at 7 a.m., one of your first priorities, after you had been detailed your day's duty, was breakfast. The mobile patrols would take it in turns, so there was always someone out there for urgent calls. One of the patrol crews were in having their breakfast one morning, when they got a call to a burglary at a house. The house itself was in a 'safe' area, which would be on the loyalist side of the fence. Not a place you would generally expect to come under attack. There is no doubt you were slightly more relaxed than in a republican area, where you could come under gun or bomb attack at any minute. Probably for that reason the call wasn't checked back to confirm that it was genuine, which would have been standard practice in a more dangerous area. You would have at least three people in the crew, which fortunately in this case was an armoured Land Rover, or Hotspur as they were known. The crew that day was made up of the driver, the observer and an extra observer, who would carry a rifle or submachine gun to give cover to the observer while he dealt with the call, and to act as a deterrent to any attackers.

As they arrived at the terraced house, the observer just jumped out and knocked the door. It was early morning and the street was very quiet. As he did so, a gunman opened fire from the other end of the street, shooting him in the stomach. The gunman continued to fire at him as he lay defenceless on the ground. The street was overlooked by a republican area and they were shooting from an upstairs flat behind the peace wall. Fortunately for him, the driver was a fairly experienced peeler and they were in a bulletproof Land Rover. He drove the vehicle up on to the footpath, putting it between the gunman and his wounded colleague. Undoubtedly his quick thinking saved his life. He hadn't been wearing his bulletproof vest. The scrambled egg he'd had for his breakfast was all over his tunic, all mixed with his blood and insides. The person who was wounded is a really great person. He's a Christian and he told me afterwards he thought he was going to die, but that he was quite happy to do so. I'm not a Christian myself but I remember thinking, that must have been a great comfort to him. I'd have been shitting myself!

When he had recovered some months later, I was out on patrol with him on his first day back to work. I'm sure it was a strange feeling for him being back in the area where he had so very nearly died. If he was nervous, he didn't show it. He was driving that night, and I was observer. We were out taking calls, as normal, in a soft-skin vehicle [not bulletproof]. We were driving past Ardoyne shop fronts, a very republican area, when we saw a group of youths acting suspiciously outside one of the shops. He decided, quite correctly, to turn the car and drive past them again to see what they were up to. As we drove up level to them, they scattered so quickly, it was unbelievable. That's never a good sign. No children in the street is another bad sign. I was convinced we were fucked. I just pulled the front of my bulletproof vest up to cover my head, and the back of it round to cover my side, and waited on the shots, as we drove like hell to get away. The shots didn't come, but it was one of those times when five seconds lasts a year and a half.

Peace

In the good old bad old days there was some pressure. My early days in the police, I didn't go into the city centre. You were always checking over your shoulder, checking under your car. Looking for trouble or things out of place. You like to think you aren't affected, but there was one day I was lying in the bath, there was a knock at the bathroom door. I heard footsteps. I got out of the bath and I ran bollock-naked up the hall. I thought, 'If I get shot, keep running.' I ran as fast as I could into the kitchen. I slipped, fell and crashed into the oven.

I just thought, 'Get up, get up.' The thought of getting shot empty-handed horrified me. So if boys come down to get me, at least I've a gun and can fight back. I would rather die fighting. I made it to my gun and I was pointing it at my kitchen door. I searched everywhere. There was nobody in the house. What had happened was a toilet roll had fallen off the top shelf in the hot press on to the landing and banged against the door. Then boom-boom-boom-boom, as the whole pile of them fell individually. In my head, there was someone running up the hall. It was just as real as that. Other people can hear a noise and think, 'What was that?' Other people can get in their car and they don't look under it. That's their normal. At that time, my normal was get my gun and investigate. Although I must admit, I did have a bit of a laugh at myself when I worked it out – but really you should be getting help.

See after the ceasefire? It was coming off the high that was the hard bit. Trying to wind back down to normal. Trying to get to sleep at night without a bottle of wine. There wasn't as much camaraderie in the job any more. It was coming off the high, that was the hardest thing.

Acknowledgements

I would like to thank my friends and former colleagues who so generously gave of their time to share their experiences with me. I know it wasn't always easy for some of you to relive the horrors of what you saw, or to say out loud things that you normally never speak of.

We all agreed that the history of Northern Ireland's troubled past and our place in it was being rewritten without our involvement – so getting our accounts on record was a catalyst for me when I started writing down my experiences and gathering together those of other officers. The resolve to put their experiences into a book was the driving force for those who found it difficult to revisit those times. As some of the perpetrators of the Troubles' most horrific acts of violence attempt to recast the events of their murderous campaign for their own ends, we RUC members are determined that our account of our direct experiences should not be overlooked or forgotten. This book will allow our story, told in our own words, to live on.

To everyone I had the honour of serving with, thank you. It was tight at times, but the craic was great.

Finally, thank you, Gill – you managed to keep me focused when other work got in the way and got me back to the job in hand. Thanks also to Lynda, whose support was invaluable, and, of course, thanks to Johanna and Rebecca, who nudged me along with a certain quietness when needed, and of whom I could not be more proud.

ABOUT THE AUTHOR

Colin Breen is a freelance journalist, screenwriter and broadcaster. He has written extensively for many newspapers, including the *Belfast Telegraph*, *Sunday Life* and *Herald Dublin*, and is a regular commentator on local and national radio, television and the BBC World Service. He served as an officer in the RUC for over fourteen years at the height of the Troubles.